SLEIGHTOF**HAND**

SLEIGHTOF**HAND**

Conversations
with
Walter
SATTERTHWAIT

Walter **SATTERTHWAIT**
and
Ernie **BULOW**

University of New Mexico Press
A l b u q u e r q u e

To
Gaye Brown
&
Ada Rutledge
Two savvy ladies who know how to tell the players

Library of Congress Cataloging-in-Publication Data

Satterthwait, Walter.
  Sleight of hand: conversations with Walter
Satterthwait / Walter Satterthwait and Ernie Bulow.—
1st ed.
      p.   cm.
  Includes bibliographical references (p.).
  ISBN 0-8263-1466-X
  1. Satterthwait, Walter—Interviews. 2. Detective
and mystery stories—Authorship. I. Bulow, Ernie,
1943–   . II. Title.
PS3569.A784Z474   1993   93-29925
813'.54—dc20   CIP

Contents

The **Search for** Walter**Satterthwait** and **the** Santa Fe Experience

All writers are magicians, illusionists who briefly breathe life into places that never were, choreograph actions that never happened, chronicle deeds both stirring and mean by people who never existed. Some merely perfect a few shabby card tricks and fool our senses with mirrors and smoke and misdirection. But how we love to be tricked, and how thrilling it is to encounter one of the great illusionists, a Houdini of the printed page, a Blackstone of the written word, a writer who, in the flamboyant style of Siegfried and Roy, can float live elephants over the heads of the audience and make raging lions disappear into the pockets of a gaudy costume.

Perhaps nowhere else in literature is the writer so obviously put into the role of prestidigitator as in the mystery genre, where the author is required to flummox us with sleight of word and misdirection and is penalized for not being wizard enough to outwit his readers and provide a suitable surprise. How delighted I am when I encounter a writer who can provide a suitable puzzle, trick it out in plenty of action, dazzle me with his legerdemain without sacrificing character or setting or the normal demands of good writing, and, on top of all that, transcend the genre in some way. If Walter Satterthwait hasn't already accomplished all that, notably in *Miss Lizzie,* he certainly shows the promise to do so. It is no accident that I fell on the metaphor of novelist as magician, because Walter's next historical mystery will feature the inimitable Harry Houdini, teaming up with his scribbling counterpart, A. Conan Doyle. The two men, both geniuses in their own way, shared a common interest in spiritualism and, though the Jewish Houdini was quick to debunk the shabby tricks of charlatan mediums and the dour Brit, Doyle, with his scientific medical background, prided himself on clear thinking and solid logic, they both hoped in vain that the spirit world would reveal itself to them.

Conan Doyle's greatest achievement was, of course, the creation of that most cerebral of detectives, Sherlock Holmes. But Holmes, who has a life of his own, it seems, was the ultimate eccentric. He did drugs, spurned women, alienated almost everyone around him with his morbid brooding and his violin playing, and loved—almost as much as solving a good puzzle—dressing up in exotic disguises to confound the senses of the enemy and fool his best and only friend, Watson. A potent combination indeed: the detective as illusionist to team up with the prestidigitating sleuth and ultimate escape artist.

Stage magic and the mystery novel have a far deeper and more fundamental connection than that of illusion and deception as entertainment, however. Behind the wizardry of a David Copperfield dematerializing a brick wall on television while millions of viewers look on and try to puzzle out the trick is a more basic and pervasive belief that magic really exists, that on some level, the supernatural can be contacted, manipulated. It is the sense of the power of that unseen world that gives us a frisson of delicious fear when we brush against it. In the realms of magic there are many objects of great power: precious metals, rare gems, exotic herbs, and the body parts of fabled creatures, saints, and members of the opposite sex. Certain geographical places are imbued with special powers, healing waters, restorative mudbaths, and airs that rehabilitate. The movements of Mars, the darks of the moon, the falling away of the seasons, the balance of day to night all have magical significance. But the demiurge, the catalyst, the cosmic glue is the ultimate power of the word.

Metals and elements, gods and demigods, prime numbers and planets, all seem to reduce to symbols and those runes and glyphs and ancient alphabets in turn to vocal utterance—The Word. Whether we consciously believe in the magic of the word or not, the proof of its potency and ultimate destructive or creative power confronts us almost every minute of every day from a careless oath to defuse the pain of a mashed finger to the fervent, heartfelt prayer of Sunday service, to the casual—but deadly serious—manipulation of our collective mind by television commercials, news media, and politicians, not necessarily in that order. The power of the word underlies all magic, the potency of the name imbues all objects, and the ability to manipulate words on the printed page or otherwise confers great gifts as well as exacting heavy penalties.

While we may long to know the secrets of some of Houdini's greatest illusions—and they may be had, alas, for a price—what we really want to know was what he thought when he took the surprise blow that killed him, how he really felt about his mother, why he was driven to push himself constantly to risk death. Most of us are endlessly curious about what makes people tick, especially the great and famous, the geniuses, the movers and shakers and shouters whom the rest of us choose to follow for one reason or another.

I don't think it is surprising at all that a great number of habitual readers, myself certainly included, are endlessly fascinated by writers, their work habits, their personal quirks, their lives, and their ideas— what they think about and why. Some of us only want to know more about the individual whose work we admire; others hope to have the author finally reveal the secret of writing so we can do it too (and be rich and famous and admired by our peers). All of us, to some extent, simply look for validation. I am always pleased to find that someone I admire thinks the way I do, has had similar experiences and reacted in the same way, especially if that response seems to be contrary to the majority voice. How happy I am when I find that some kooky notion that has been juggling around in my brain for years, supressed by fears of ridicule or noncomprehension, has similarly been niggling around in the mind of someone intelligent and even successful.

So even though I have read the biographies of several dozen writers over the years, sat through all those college classes on the hollow promise of illumination, slogged through silly "How-to-Write-Like-Joseph Conrad-and-Sell-Like-Judith Krantz" books, and read reams of magazine articles by authors who obviously had no idea what really made them successful but were gratified and appreciative that success had sought them out— even given all of that—I still enjoy the company of writers and still keep asking the same questions, hoping for that moment of epiphany, that mental cry of "Eureka!" that means I've finally got it. Actually, I'm not so sure I really want to get it. I already know most of the answers. Most successful writers share a handful of traits and life-styles. On the glamorous side is a short list including a questioning mind, a restless nature, an independent turn of thought. On the practical side are hard, solitary work and self-discipline—the grim reality that writing, like most successful jobs, requires forty or more hours a week, fifty or more weeks a year. Not what we wanted to know at all.

I first met Walter Satterthwait shortly after he had finished writing his second hardcover, the first of his historical mysteries, *Miss Lizzie.* We were both attending a luncheon meeting of an informal organization known as First Friday, which was started by Tony Hillerman, Norman Zollinger, and a few of their friends. The first Friday of each month a small group of writers gather in Albuquerque to shoot the breeze over lunch, exchange literary gossip, pass around copies of their latest efforts, and get out of the house and away from the word processor for a couple of hours. The only requirement for "membership" is to be a published author. In New Mexico that includes a large collection of folks, and that particular day I couldn't get a seat anywhere near Tony, though we had come into the restaurant together. I found myself sitting between a heavyset older man with a florid complexion and a slender, dark, dashingly handsome fellow I guessed to be a couple of years younger than I. The older man introduced himself as R. D. Brown, and I was immensely relieved that I had just read—and enjoyed—his book *Hazzard,* first of the Cheney Hazzard mysteries set in Brownsville, Texas. It was a paperback original and nominated for an Edgar Award. We chatted a bit over lunch and the slender fellow on the other side of me seemed a bit too quiet for the company he was in. In the natural course of things I got around to introducing myself to him and I discovered I'd just read *his* first novel, *Wall of Glass,* and enjoyed it a great deal. It was a day for pleasant coincidences.

Phoenix bookseller Russ Todd had traded me a copy of *Wall of Glass* for a copy of Carl Hiassen's first solo effort, *Tourist Season,* which I had gotten personally inscribed for him at a writers' conference in Key West. I thought I'd been had, as usual, on a lopsided trade. "The book is set in Santa Fe," he told me. "You'll love it." Another strike against it, being told I had to like it, but I was interested in the New Mexico background.

Wall of Glass was not a disappointment. I knew we had a promising new writer to read and enjoy if he could repeat his success and build on it. The book was pretty formulaic: wiseass detective playing Archie Goodwin by doing the legwork for an intelligent handicapped female Hispanic. Satterthwait's Joshua Croft was a tough pragmatist who took a quixotic moral stance somewhere in the company of White Knights like Travis McGee, who had a friend in the police department to run license plates for him, who could fight, drive dangerous mountain roads, spurn unwanted female advances, and so on. Satterthwait made effective, if sparing, use of the Santa Fe setting, and some of that, like the glitzy art gallery scene, was a tad strained by traditional cliche. The Hispanic godfather in his retreat high in the Sangre de Cristo mountains toward Taos was a nice touch, too. But what I really loved, the thing that lifted the book above the genre by several degrees, was the wit and effective use of language. Years later I still chuckle at Walter's definition of chorizo as "red dye #8 and parts of the pig its mother wouldn't recognise" to paraphrase loosely from memory.

Besides being rather better written and more stylish than the average for the genre, *Wall of Glass* turned out to be much better plotted than I had expected, delivering a couple of nice twists at the end and an ultimate villain who was not only a total surprise (don't tell me *you* figured it out) but epitomized someone with all the advantages who has managed to grow up without a soul. I liked the book, liked what the author was up to.

Funny I hadn't noticed the resemblance between the tall, skinny guy I was sitting next to at lunch and the elegant, lanky figure on the dust jacket of *Wall of Glass.* Conversation drifted about a bit, touching on his as-yet-unpublished novel *Miss Lizzie.* He promised me a review copy, which never materialized. Satterthwait mentioned that he'd written the book in Thailand, of all places, and the next time I heard his name mentioned he was in Greece or Africa or someplace exotic. He never seemed to be in Santa Fe.

Partly out of pique at not getting my freebie, I didn't pick up a copy of *Miss Lizzie* when it first came out, even though I had enjoyed his earlier work. When rumors started circulating that this was perhaps a minor masterpiece I discovered that there were no first printings anywhere. Everyone in the trade, dealers and collectors of modern firsts, knows that anything but a first state of the first printing of a book is merely a reading copy. Everyone in the book business but me already seemed to know that this Walter Satterthwait was a hot property, and I found out that *Wall of Glass* was already fetching fifty dollars and more. Luckily I had picked up a few copies of that book, but I had to pay thirty dollars for a first of *Miss Lizzie* after a specialist bookseller read me the opening page in a voice of respectful awe at his skill as a writer. "Can you believe how perfectly he picks up the point of view of a young girl?" she asked me. For some reason I still didn't read the book, even after paying a premium for it and holding still for various testimonials on Walter's behalf. Then the second book of the Joshua Croft series came out. I bought ten copies and read one of them immediately. The promise of the first Santa Fe book was more than fulfilled by the second, which was richer in characterization, setting, plot, and everything else that mattered. His old Indian fellow was damned good too, and I'm pretty critical of that sort of thing. But there was no attempt whatsoever to poach on Tony Hillerman's preserve. It was a solid series detective novel with all the trappings and conventions of the genre, but with some superior writing and a wise-talking detective who was a cross between Fletch and Phillip Marlowe. Pretty good stuff. Now he introduced another detective more in the tradition of the Continental Op, Hammett's nameless detective who reveals very little about himself (he narrates the stories he appears in) except that he is short and fat. More about him later.

With *At Ease with the Dead* sitting so comfortably on my shelf I went back and picked up *Miss Lizzie*—finally. I was a little skeptical about liking a historical mystery featuring a famous hatchet killer and told from the point of view of a prepubescent girl. I was immediately caught up in the book, its precocious yet charming narrator, its excellent characterization, the seedy, underrated agency detective (another nod to Hammett's Continental Op) and especially the wonderful old woman, Lizzie Borden herself. I was troubled by the fact that I was getting to like Lizzie so much, not really knowing anything about the historical character, but assuming she had, indeed, committed a couple of grisly murders on her own parents. What relief to have one of the characters tell the narrator that Lizzie Borden had actually been acquitted of the bloody deed in real life. The relief was short-lived, however, when it became obvious that Satterthwait meant to tell the reader that she had, in fact, hacked up both her parents years before—a sort of pact of understanding between the young girl and the old woman, a symbol of their special relationship, a deadly secret of sorts. The girl is not appalled by this revelation, but seems to accept and understand it in some special way. The problem for me was that I couldn't understand what Satterthwait was up to. Clearly, the woman was guilty, and yet he never tried to explain the circumstances, mitigate the act on some moral or even practical ground. He wasn't going to make excuses for the woman at all, and that left me in what I considered a moral dilemma—liking a "bad" person rather a lot and not being given an excuse to forgive her the sins of the past.

I badly wanted to talk to Walter Satterthwait at this point, but I couldn't find him. Since the drive from Gallup to Albuquerque is an incredibly boring trip of two hours plus and Tony Hillerman and other prominent writers seldom show up at First Friday these days, I hadn't been to a meeting in rather a long time. At this point I needed to get some books signed by Judith Van Gieson, one of the best of the new women mystery writers and a New Mexican a good part of each year, and I heard she had been attending the lunches so I dropped by the Indian Pueblo Cultural Center where the group had been gathering lately.

Talking Mysteries had gone through three printings and very respectable sales at this point and was widely reviewed in fairly favorable terms so I was playing with the idea of doing similar books with other authors I knew. I really wanted to use writers that I already had some acquaintance and rapport with, or at least authors whose work I admired and had some emotional, philosophical and intellectual ties with. I was also looking for a Southwestern connection, if possible, so the University of New Mexico Press would be interested. The truth is, *Talking Mysteries* wasn't really their kind of book but it had Tony Hillerman's name on it. I finally caught up with Walter at the First Friday lunch and he was quick to accept my proposal to do a book similar to *Talking Mysteries,* which I was delighted to find he had actually read and liked, appreciating—he said—my total candor and honesty. Always easy to appreciate candor when you're not the subject of it. He also knew, almost as soon as I did, that the book had been nominated for a Mystery Writers of America Edgar Award in the biographical/critical category. Walter, in spite of having seven books behind him and some degree of critical success, is still among the undiscovered as far as those massive sales that free man's soul are concerned. Like a lot of contemporary writers these days, Satterthwait appreciates his public and tries to do any book signings he gets requests for. He is also becoming active with several of the fan conventions like Bouchercon where a writer actually gets to meet his readers. Partly because he has ties to New York he is active with the Mystery Writers of America, keeps in touch with the organization and was on one of the award panels that year. At any rate he encouraged me to attend the big annual banquet and bask in the glow of my nomination. Also, he was going to be in New York on his way to Europe and liked to attend the Edgars.

I travel a great deal when I'm in my trader persona, working Indian shows, book fairs, and similar events. For various reasons I spend a lot of time in Santa Fe, a place I enjoy very much in spite of its arty pretensions and carnival atmosphere. There is a benign air to Santa Fe that I don't feel in similar places. Tourist towns like Aspen and Jackson have a nasty, grasping, screw-outsiders feel, a barely suppressed air of greed and envy and corruption. In Santa Fe things are more laid back, more humorous— more cultured, if you will. The place has a life independent from the tourists. For the initiated it is a town of rare and wonderful possibilities. It has, for example, more antiquarian booksellers per capita than any place in the world. And of the hundreds of art galleries a dozen or so are owned and run by intelligent people of good taste who promote real art and exciting new artists as well as the established greats. Regardless of its faults, Santa Fe is beautifully situated geographically and has a nearly perfect climate, and the multicultural atmosphere of Hispanic, Indian and Old West elements has been a magnet for painters and writers for more than a century.

Walter Satterthwait has been in and out of Santa Fe for some years now, until recently supporting himself by tending bar, a career he has great fondness for. A gypsy nomad, Walter keeps his worldly possessions to an absolute minimum, and the cramped, two-story apartment where we taped most of our interviews wasn't likely to impress anybody. The twisting cast-iron staircase which connected his tiny bedroom/kitchenette with the writing studio above was barely wide enough to pass my current bulk, and Walter kept the air blue with tobacco smog as he chainsmoked low-tar cigarettes he bought a pack at a time from overpriced vending machines. His charming landlady turned out to be Ada Rutledge, one of the Grande Dames of Southwestern letters whose name is linked, romantically and otherwise, to many of the literary names of New Mexico including Frank Waters and Max Evans. She knew most of the leading figures of the golden age of Taos and Santa Fe and tells a great story with dry wit and self-deprecating charm.

Interviewing Satterthwait turned out to be much harder than taping Tony Hillerman. I had known Tony for years, spent time in his home, hung around him at conferences and, partly thanks to his bibliographer Louis Heib, had a fat file of articles on him. And I had been reading and selling his books for years so I was pretty familiar with them. Hillerman had suffered innumerable interviews by the time the two of us sat down to talk and, to be truthful, had a number of incidents and aspects of his life already buffed and polished for public inspection. He has, in the course of two decades of interviews and articles, a repertoire of personal anecdotes that he trots out for journalists with the ease and amiability of the country storyteller he is. For my part, I knew the questions to ask and was thoroughly familiar with the Four Corners Country and Navajo culture. Almost every minute of our three hours of tape yielded usable, interesting material which took relatively little editing. An hour of biography, two hours of patter on words, weather, and wolfmen.

Walter has not yet endured the tedium of repeating the same answers to the same old questions year after year, anticipating the needs of critic/reviewer/biographer with thought-out, predigested statements of purpose and direction, aims and aspirations and pet peeves. For my part, I was more inclined to interrupt Walter, put words in his mouth, direct the line of questioning astray, and otherwise destroy his train of thought. The fact is, we just had too much fun talking to one another, discovering the pleasure of shared convictions, favorite books and authors, similar travels, wandering hither and yon as the subject led us. In the end I had eight hours on tape, much of that difficult to transcribe because we moved around the cramped apartment and forgot the tape recorder for stretches of time, often not knowing how long it had been stopped, out of tape, while the two of us jawed on.

There were an equal number of hours of discussion during my several visits to Santa Fe that spring which simply didn't get on tape at all, much of which didn't deserve to be recorded anyway, I'm sure. So much energy and discussion was devoted to airing our likes and dislikes, bashing false reputations, bolstering egos, or simply following lines of thought that had relatively little interest to anyone but us that it was very difficult to organize and edit the tapes at all. The process was made even more difficult by the fact that, just as we were getting to know each other and be comfortable with the whole thing, Walter had to leave for Amsterdam and a house-sitting gig where he will write his next Joshua Croft mystery, which deals with the myriad New Age alternative healers in the Southwest, each chapter being tied to a card in the Tarot deck—what could be more Santa Fe? In the end, Walter's final editing of his side of the conversations took place on several airplane flights through Europe.

A week before he left for Europe, Walter and friends Jonathan Richards and Claudia Jessup gave a reading from his not-yet-published *A Flower in the Desert,* which has Croft investigating a famous actor accused of child molesting whose ex-wife's flight becomes intertwined with a tale of terrorist activities in Nicaragua. A small but interesting group of fans gathered at Old Santa Fe Trail Books, the only bookstore I've ever seen with a liquor license. The three-voice dramatic rendering of two chapters of the book was really a treat. The week before, Walter and I had searched for a copy shop open on Sunday so he could give me his copy of the manuscript to read. Santa Fe is not exactly a Sunday closing town and we found a place not far from the Zia Diner on Guadalupe. The service was typically lackadaisical, and a youngish woman with improbably red hair and one eye that drifted slightly finally waited on us with a pained air. Walter explained which chapters he needed three copies of and the bored clerk immediately launched into a singsong recitation of selections from the international copyright law. Walter, ever the gentleman, held up a slender hand and said politely, "I *am* the author," which ground the girl's presentation to a halt. She looked him up and down, momentarily bringing both eyes to bear, and sneered, "Oh, another writer," as though such creatures hounded her days and infested the local woodwork. I guess there are a lot of writers in Santa Fe.

Between taping sessions Walter and I did a bit of bar hopping to soothe our parched throats, hitting such notable local watering holes as the Bull Ring, Vanessie's, the Palace Bar, the Coyote Cafe, and Evangelo's, which serves every beer in the world except Budweiser. I had been in all those places many times before, and maybe a few others as well, but visiting taverns with a man who is a legend in the local bartending mythology is a real treat. He is a celebrity to a horde of locals who have no idea he ever wrote a book and wouldn't—perhaps couldn't—read it anyway. There is something very seductive about celebrity no matter what it is based on. One evening, looking for a late meal, we hit the San Francisco Bar and Grill and discovered a long line in spite of the hour. All good eateries in Santa Fe exact this toll, like a rite of passage. One has to wait to eat. Once Walter caught the eye of the fellow impersonating a maitre d' we were whisked to a table in the heavy smoking section and seated immediately. I tried to feel remorseful for this special treatment—dozens of people were glaring at us—but I could only feel that glow of celebrity perk. Now if Walter can just become as famous as a writer as he is a bartender he'll have it made.

We both worked hard during our interview sessions to come up with material that would be interesting to the reader, but Walter's natural shyness kept certain subject matter at bay, and his lack of practice with the literary interview situation is obvious—I asked him a lot of questions he hadn't had occasion to think about before. It became obvious that, given more time, years of acquaintance, some wonderful stuff would come out. It was hard for Walter to pin down sources of scenes and characters and bits from his books, aside from the obviously researched ones like *Miss Lizzie* and *Wilde West*. I knew the stories were there, but didn't know how to tap into them. I seem to be the last bookman in America to know that Walter had two paperback originals published back in the early eighties by Dell, one set in New York, dealing with drugs, and one set on a Greek island, dealing with drugs. The first, *Cocaine Blues,* is a well-crafted, snappy read with a couple of fine scenes. Walter was drawing heavily on his years as a bartender in Manhattan. In *The Aegean Affair* the tale is more formulaic but still certainly readable with one of his better female characters and a second-string hero who, unfortunately, gets killed off and is thus unavailable for sequels. In the Greek book there is a scene where the hero shoots a hired killer through his hotel window with a spear gun. Walter is an experienced snorkeler and skin diver and tells elsewhere of spearing his dinner most afternoons between writing stints on an African island. Two of his short stories deal with skin diving as well.

While we were discussing *The Aegean Affair* Satterthwait was frustrated by my nagging for good anecdotes about his several trips to Greece, the writing of the book, or anything else interesting. During several of our weekends together either Gaye Brown or I had been shooting a lot of photos of Walter for use in the book, and for the dust jacket of *A Flower in the Desert.* Walter is a little vain about his lean good looks, and we shot more film than we might have to be sure we got some good stuff—also knowing he'd be inaccessible for several months. He told us the story of his passport photo—good for ten years—which showed him with a swollen, ravaged nose, the result of an accident with a spear gun. On one of his visits to Greece, while writing one of his books set somewhere else, he ran out of money, a situation hardly novel in his experience. After several days with little or no food, he happened to spy a rabbit outside his window. Naively, he picked up the only weapon at hand and threw off a shot. He didn't even scare the rabbit, but the unexpected recoil of the spear gun, which he had only fired underwater before, took a big chunk out of his nose. Of course I used this tale as proof that Walter had a lot of amusing or enlightening anecdotes tucked away somewhere in memory if we could just root them out. Sadly, that obvious example didn't help much.

An even more tantalizing incident occurred on our last evening in New York City as Walter led us through some of his old haunts in and around Greenwich Village. We stopped in the Lion's Head, a well-known literary hangout with Bass ale on tap and dust jackets papering the walls. Every writer who ever hung out there had a book represented, it seems, and before the evening was over Satterthwait had been added to the roster, which seemed to please him as much as if he had just been nominated for the Nobel. A dust cover from one of Kinky Friedman's books was sandwiched between two forgettable titles and I mentioned being fond of his music. Kinky Friedman and the Texas Jewboys from Kerrville, Texas, home of the Cowboy Artists of America museum. Walter looked at me in disbelief, "You know who Kinky Friedman is?" Of course it turned out that Kinky was one of Walter's old drinking buddies from his New York days, and, if he'd only thought of it, there were some great stories there. Maybe for another book.

One obvious question will be asked about this book that never came up with Tony Hillerman and that, of course, is why a book on Walter Satterthwait, especially so early in his career. Naturally I have a good answer to that; several of them in fact. For one thing, Walter's perception of himself is bound to change as he gets more successful and more famous, and he's bound to do both. At this point in his career he's still feeling things out, still testing the current, so to speak, still under the thumb of his publisher to a certain extent, still forced to depend on the kindness of strangers. I don't think there is any question that Walter Satterthwait has some great books in him, but he is at a crisis point in his career. As he discusses elsewhere, his publisher would only allow him to do *Miss Lizzie* if he promised to deliver another Joshua Croft book, and he is currently punching away at the third series mystery in a row while the brilliant if confusing *Wilde West* languishes in the warehouse. Critics mostly loved the book, as I did, but fans have been very tentative about it and the publisher is sure that the series is the direction Satterthwait should go, since a successful series has a built-in audience. Walter would currently like to move back and forth, feeling that the offbeat novels, the mysteries he calls "sports," polish his skills, refresh his skull, push at the boundaries of the genre. I believe that his literary reputation will rest with the nonseries books; *Miss Lizzie* is already being recognized as a major achievement.

Mysteries set in the past using famous people who really existed have been done successfully by several mystery writers. Satterthwait's are more than a fictional recreation of the past. Walter uses novelistic freedom to bring characters together in unlikely combinations—Oscar Wilde, Doc Holliday, Jack the Ripper, and Baby Doe Tabor, for example—and then a little revisionist history for spice (what if Holliday were gay and Wilde straight, for example) and then combining those elements with the conventions of the contemporary crime novel: sex, graphic violence, ambiguous morality, loose chronology, and nontraditional plot. In the case of *Wilde West* there was a special element in the choice of Oscar Wilde as a central character because it took a lot of nerve (some might even say outrageous egotism) to put words in the mouth of one of the great wits of history. It is one of the real triumphs of *Wilde West* that Wilde's speeches are perfect and unstrained. The graphic horror of the marshal's discovery of the flayed prostitute's grinning skull face is an image that will stick with me for years to come.

If *Wilde West* is such a brilliant tour-de-force why are sales sluggish and many fans lukewarm if not repelled and even outraged? Mystery readers are a somewhat conservative lot, which is the central reason for the exploding popularity of the genre at the moment. With modern literature drifting every closer to plotless, structureless, characterless exercises in the brilliant use of language, the mystery form exerts a strong appeal in the direction of formal development, conventional plotting, adherence to various predictable conventions—introducing the murderer early in the story, playing fair with clues, clearcut right and wrong and so on—and the general comfort of familiarity. *Wilde West* violates several of those conventions, especially regarding the ambiguous moral positions of several major characters. In other words, it's just a bit too much for many readers. I predict that a few years from now this will be one of the most sought after of Satterthwait's books and something of a landmark in the genre.

All in all, this book may raise more questions than it can answer, but I hope it will be a provocative look at the early career of a major talent in the genre—though such things are always hard to call. At least it should be a treat for Satterthwait's growing number of fans and, if nothing else, it makes available a couple of his early short stories and one rather gothic tale which has never seen publication before. Enjoy.

Walter Satterthwait:
A Biography in Dialogue

Walter Satterthwait was born in Bryn Mawr, Pennsylvania, on March 23, 1946, the eldest of five children. He lived up and down the East Coast as a child: Ithaca, Syracuse, Mamaroneck, and New Rochelle, New York; Milford and Orange, Connecticut; Baltimore, Maryland; and then, on his own at eighteen, New York City.

He managed to not graduate from high school, and though he attended Reed College in Portland, Oregon, for several years, off and on, he managed to avoid graduation there as well. Though he has always worked at writing, he supported himself for twenty years mostly as a bartender or club manager, night work that kept him close to booze and women, interesting people, odd working hours, and exotic places.

He is a rather private person who is reluctant to reveal much of his personal side unless it relates directly to his writing. With his seventh book about to be released he is just able, now, to live on his writing income alone and consider himself an established author. He just recently got to know a grown daughter he had never met, Jennifer, twenty-two, and is experiencing fatherhood for the first time, with no Pampers to change or bottles to fix.

Most of his books have been written in exotic corners of the world where he can escape the demands of family and friends and shrieking telephones, live frugally in solitude, and maintain the rigorous routine and self-discipline required to produce a novel. This nomadic existence keeps his possessions, relationships, and other encumbrances to a minimum.

We tried to make the biography a coherent, cohesive whole, but a great deal of biographical information is scattered through the other interviews as well, so there is probably some inadvertent repetition. The conversations recorded here took place over a period of six weeks.

EB: Most writers I know or read about seem to have crafted their biographies toward their ultimate vocation. The marks of the writer first appear in early childhood; they tend to be loners, daydreamers, indifferent students, they tend to be restless, moving around a lot, changing jobs, often feeling alienated—it almost sounds like the lyrics to a country-western tune: "Mommas, don't let your babies grow up to be writers."

WS: I knew I wanted to be a writer by the time I was twelve. It comes from reading, I think, and I was reading before kindergarten. I was lucky. I was the first of five children and my mother had time to read to me that she didn't have with the other kids. And from the time I can remember being conscious, I was reading, always. Everything. Books, newspapers, cereal boxes.

EB: So you always worked in that direction.

WS: I wanted to get involved with science initially. All the aptitude tests I took in school pointed me that way. I scored fairly high in English, but I scored higher in the sciences. I loved biology, geology, natural science. Rocks, plants, animals. Great stuff. And physics. I thought nuclear fission was terrific. I remember, for one science project, I built a model of a nuclear reactor. It didn't actually work, of course, because I couldn't get my hands on any real U-235. But I had the theory down pretty well. I'm surprised I wasn't strafed by the U.S. Air Force.

But when I was around twelve, it occurred to me, mostly from my reading about writers of the thirties and forties, that the writing life seemed very glamorous. More glamorous than the scientific life. You stayed up late, you hung out with beautiful women. Scientists were in bed by eight and they were usually married to women named Martha, who were probably good cooks but who never wore lace corsets and fishnet stockings. You can see that I came by my superficiality fairly early on.

And, as a writer, you wouldn't have to have an alarm clock, the sound of which, the *thought* of which, I hated. At that point in school, homework had begun to be assigned and I'd lost whatever interest I had in the educational process. These people were already taking eight hours of my life, five days a week, and now they wanted to pilfer some of my time at home as well. And, in order to submit myself to this theft, I had to get up in the morning, before the chickens. Totally unfair, it seemed to me. When you're a writer, or so I thought, you don't have to have an alarm clock. *And* you get to travel a lot. By then my family had already moved up and down the East Coast, which made it difficult for me to set down roots but which consequently, I think, was probably the reason I came to like, and to this day still like, the idea of travel. I keep looking for that next place, which may be *the* place: Brigadoon, Shangri La, Peoria. . . . So I knew what I wanted to do by the time I was twelve. On balance, though, it was mostly the alarm clock.

EB: Were you a closet writer or were you looking for an audience at an early age?

WS: In junior high I got some stuff published in the school magazine and I sent some stuff to the comic books. I thought I had some great ideas for the comics, swell stuff involving dinosaurs or severed limbs, or maybe it was dinosaurs with severed limbs, which in retrospect is maybe not an especially commercial idea. I wrote to them outlining these masterpieces, but they never wrote back. My first rejection. I recall waiting for a letter from this guy and I don't think I wrote anything after that for a long time because I never heard from him. It was wounding. An editor at E-C comics, this guy was. Those were the comics that caused the big shakeup in the fifties. They were banned. Great scary stuff, skulls and bones and severed limbs. Even some dinosaurs. But not dinosaurs with severed limbs, unfortunately.

EB: I probably remember the old E-C line better than you do. The only title of theirs that survived the great Dr. Wertham congressional shakeup of the fifties was *Mad*. I can see touches of that tongue-in-cheek brand of horror as a thread through your work. Aside from your budding writing career, what kind of student were you?

WS: Lazy. I aced it. I did as little homework as I had to do to get by, up until high school, when I stopped doing even that. I hated school. From about the fifth grade on it was a prison and I hated it. It was boring and stupid and my time wasn't mine, it belonged to somebody else.

But I can tell you, apropos of school, where part of my fondness for mystery writing comes in. This happened in the fifth grade. There was one teacher, a woman, enormously fat, who was sort of prowling around the tables in the school cafeteria at lunchtime. Now, at that time the kids were allowed to take all the food they wanted off the cafeteria line. I don't know if that's still true. Anyway, this sixth grader—an elder, of course, as far as I was concerend, because at that time I was only a fifth grader— had his whole tray piled high with stuff, and he was sitting at the table and he was about to dig in. And then this woman comes up to him and says, "You look like you're expecting a famine."

And he turns to her and he says, "You look like you caused one."

I thought that was terrific. I mean, first of all, even if this woman had been a bloody wood nymph who weighed only ninety-five pounds, it was none of her business what this guy was eating. But the fact was, she had clearly, over the years, eaten more than her fair share herself. More than anyone's fair share. More than the fair share of a medium-sized municipality. Where did she get off trying to put *him* down?

There's a price to pay, though, for wit. I heard the kid got suspended. But if I'd been him, I'd have thought it was worth it. It was a good line.

That kind of humor—put-down, wiseass humor—really appealed to me. And then, when I started reading mysteries, especially in writers like Chandler, I saw that it was there. It's one of my favorite aspects of the genre.

EB: Reaching its apogee in the Gregory MacDonald "Fletch" books.

WS: Yeah. They're funny, extremely funny. You laugh out loud.

EB: That character type is a staple of the private eye subgenre—I just wish most of them could do it better. I wish I could do it better.

WS: In real life? Yeah, me too. I can always do it better after the fact. I remember the clever retorts afterwards. That's the advantage of writing, you can go back and put in all the clever stuff. You have as long as you need to work it out.

EB: Back to school. What did you do besides read?

WS: Nothing. I walked in the woods with the dog. A lot. I spent most of my early years in Connecticut, and we lived near some fair-sized stands of forest. I loved them, used to wander through them all the time. Fancied myself Chingachgook.

I was a solitary kid. I wasn't big on clubs. I joined the Cub Scouts one time, but I didn't like the den mother, or I liked her too much, I forget which. I don't think that Cub Scouts are allowed to date their den mother. That's the only group I ever belonged to.

I had a bad accident when I was twelve . . . fell out of a tree. I was doing the Tarzan number where you swing from vine to vine, but this particular tree was short on strategically placed vines and I went sailing. Fortunately, the ground broke my fall. It broke my wrists, too. I walked around like a praying mantis for a couple of months, both arms in slings. So all I did was read. Had to turn the pages carefully. I was reading everything, even poetry.

I started learning poetry because I thought it would get me somewhere with women. I had just recently discovered women—we called them *girls* back then, imagine that—and I believed that if you had all these poems memorized women would fall dead at your feet. It didn't work. I don't think I ever quoted a single poem to a woman in my life.

I take that back. My wife was Greek and I remember quoting Byron's "Maid of Athens." She was singularly unimpressed.

I was into sports, but not school sports—sandlot stuff. We had neighborhood teams for baseball and football and we took them seriously. I used to weight 225 pounds, believe it or not, when I was fourteen years old. I was about six feet tall. Maybe that's when I picked up a physical arrogance that partially explains why I'm sometimes capable of being a jerk now.

EB: You are obviously very concerned about your appearance anyway. But this thing of being a loner, often feeling like an outsider, is almost part of the paradigm of the writer's biography.

WS: Being an observer more than a participant. Yeah. Later on, when I was managing bars, I didn't like to boss people. I'm uncomfortable with it, and although I think I did a pretty good job as a bar manager, I was never very comfortable with that part of it. Not just firing, but hiring— or turning someone down for a job when they wanted it.

Anyway, after I made a sort of deliberate shift from budding scientist to budding writer, I was writing all the time. I remember once I ran out of paper. I was fifteen or sixteen. No paper in the house. So I used toilet paper, a half a roll of it, to finish whatever it was I needed to write at the moment. I just wanted to get this wonderful story down.

I didn't submit anything for years, not after the staggering disappointment of being turned down by E-C comics.

But it was a story I'd done in high school that enabled me to go to college.

EB: I sense a great writer's anecdote. Let's hear about it.

WS: I never finished high school. In the tenth grade I flunked geometry and typing. You had to really work at it to flunk typing. But I just wasn't going to class. Wasn't going to any of the classes.

My father wouldn't pay for me to go to summer school. We'd had, the two of us, an antagonistic relationship for years. His argument then was that since I'd wasted a year, I should pay for it by wasting another year. It's a logic I've never entirely understood. Summer school would've cost something like thirty dollars. Instead he spent a couple of grand to send me to this Catholic school in Pennsylvania—a boarding school— where they literally whipped kids into shape. I didn't care much for it. But, to be fair, they didn't care much for me, either. I made a point of trying to convince altar boys to become atheists. Sheer cussedness.

I came back and I was going to New Rochelle High School when my family moved again. My father was a club manager—businessmen's clubs, lunch and dinner and libraries with old guys sitting slumped behind the *Wall Street Journal* in leather chairs, and sometimes they were dead for two or three days before anyone figured it out. Anyway, he kept getting better and better club offers, so the family shifted around a lot.

They were going to Baltimore, but he was going to let me stay in New Rochelle for my senior year and finish up. I had a room in a boarding house and I was working in a grocery store. Assistant produce manager— women would come up to me and ask me if this particular cantaloupe was ripe, and I'd squeeze it and then hold it next to my ear and shake it, and I'd tell them, "Yeah, sure, this'll be perfect by Tuesday, around four o'clock." I didn't know anything about cantaloupes. What does a seventeen-year-old kid know about cantaloupes, unless he's been raised on Maui?

Anyway, my father changed his mind about my staying in New Rochelle and I had to move to Baltimore with the family. In Baltimore, the school system wouldn't accept some of my credits, some of the courses I'd taken—psychology, for example. They'd never heard of psychology. They were a little bit behind the times, educationally speaking. They did have courses in dowsing, though. And I hear that's coming back. Anyway, I learned that I'd have to repeat my eleventh-grade year.

I remember distinctly the first day of the English class, and the teacher telling us that we weren't going to worry about book reports and stuff like that. No sir. We were going to polish up the old grammar. Well, my grammar, after the year of Catholic school, was so polished that it gleamed and glistened like a Cadillac hubcap. On the third day of school, I pretended to be going there as usual, but when I got out of sight, I tossed my books in a trash can and hitchhiked to New York, where I stayed with a friend, called my mother, and told her I wasn't coming back to Baltimore. Ever. I was eighteen at the time.

EB: Hit the road and never looked back, as they say.

WS: I got a job at the New York Playboy Club because a friend of my father's was managing it. It was neat for an eighteen-year-old to be working at the Playboy Club. Maybe *neat* isn't strong enough a word. Miraculous?

A few months after I started, I moved in with a bunny, a really bright and talented woman—she was a former schoolteacher, an artist, a photographer. We lived together for about a year. Then I realized that I didn't like working for a living—laziness once again rears its ugly head—and that I really wanted to go to college.

I had taken the National Merit Exam in my junior year, and the day before the test I'd read something in *Time* magazine about Reed College in Oregon. What a neat place it was, liberal, filled with bright kids, and on the forefront of the sexual and drug revolution. Well, I was all for sex and drugs, and so, on a whim, in the section of the exam where you're supposed to put down your choice of college, I put down Reed.

After I'd been in New York for a year, Reed wrote to me, asking what had happened. Where was I? Why hadn't I followed up on my college plans?

I wrote them back and said that I'd dropped out of high school and wasn't going back, except in shackles, and maybe dead, and I asked them if maybe we could work something out, Reed and I.

Reed was terrific. They arranged an interview with a man named Howard Waskow, a professor there. We hit it off and he told me to take the SAT test and to send along a short story, if I had one. I took the SAT's and did fairly well, and I had this story I'd written about a young kid, which I sent along with my application. I'm inclined to think that it was the story that got me in.

I attended Reed for about three years, off and on. I owe the school a lot. First, they let me be there at a time when neat things were happening.

Dope. Rebellion. And free love, which was the only kind I could afford. But I liked Reed for a lot more than that. I was majoring in English, and for the first time I saw what studying—what scholarship was all about. I had a woman professor who taught a class in allegory. Catherine Smith. She was a medievalist and a first-rate teacher. It seemed to me then—still does—that the mystery genre came directly out of the medieval romances, the grail quest.

In Catherine's class, I did a paper that proved—or tried to prove—some point I wanted to make about a book called *The Romance of the Rose.* It has two authors. The first author stops and the second one continues with the same story. Scholars have always assumed the first writer stopped because he died, although there's no historical evidence to support that. I argued that the first writer stopped exactly where he wanted to stop—where he wanted to end the story—and I used an analysis of the techniques of troubadour poetry to make my case. Which I believe I did—Catherine bought it, anyway. I was proud of that. Still am.

I really enjoyed the discipline of scholarship. I liked the idea of following a trail and documenting the argument. It's not that different from what a private detective does. As Josephine Tey established in *The Daughter of Time,* one of the great mystery novels and a nifty piece of scholarship.

I was putting myself through school: I had the scholarship, and the student loans, and I worked part time in the library. Some money had been coming from my father, but he decided to withdraw that help. I left school for a while. I started selling encyclopedias part time and I did well at it. Surprisingly well, considering that basically I'm fairly shy. But I never saved a dime of the money I earned. I bought myself a fur coat, a Buick Riviera . . . toys. Self-indulgence has always been a skill that came easily to me.

So I was selling encyclopedias door to door and for a long time I really believed it was a great deal they were offering. That's probably why I was good at it. Collier's were the people who put out the encyclopedia. When I stopped believing it was a great deal, I discovered that I couldn't sell the things anymore. I was trapped, it seemed to me. I still had payments to make on the Riviera. But then the car got totaled. At first, that seemed to me like one of the great tragedies of the twentieth century—I loved that car. But then I realized that I could get out of the door-to-door business, and I went back to school.

That's when I got involved with drugs on a fairly serious basis. Grass, coke, acid, whatever. I'd been reading Rimbaud and Baudelaire and reading their biographies and thinking that this was a pretty interesting life: take drugs, screw around with glamorous women. Decadence can be enormously attractive. I was reading Burroughs, too. I was reading about drugs before they were around. And when they became available I started taking them.

I've talked this over with some friends who had been involved with drugs and with alcoholism, and it seems to me that there's usually a pattern involved in substance abuse. Usually there's some kind of personal wound that was established early within the structure of the family. There's also—clearly, I think—a physical predisposition toward addiction, a genetic inclination. And among a lot of substance abusers there's often some very early experimentation with their minds—like making themselves deliberately dizzy. Kids learn to squat, then stand up and blow on their thumbs, to make themselves faint. I did it myself—I remember thinking it was a neat way to change something, to alter the mind. So when drugs became fashionable, I lived a fashionable life.

I remember taking LSD as early as '65, when it actually wasn't all that easily obtainable—pharmaceutical LSD, from the Sandoz lab in Switzerland. And mescaline. The visions, I remember, were extraordinary with mescaline. You bring to any drug experience a certain set of presuppositions, expectations, but I remember taking mescaline on a train trip from New York when I saw a Mayan priest walk down the aisle. I was reading a John Barth story in *Esquire* and for some reason it was the funniest issue of *Esquire* I'd ever read and the Barth story was brilliant and then suddenly this Mayan priest in full headdress was marching down the aisle, rolling a huge calendar stone ahead of him.

I took that crap with virtually no religious sanctions, which is not the way to take it, if you're going to take it at all. You have to do it, I think, as part of a ritual, in something of a religious context. I took it as though I were going to the movies. I was an idiot. I later had a bad trip at college—went totally nuts—and I deserved it. You don't fuck around with your mind that way. At that age you don't believe you'll do yourself any permanent damage or o.d.—although I saw both things happen to other people. You're a buffoon—you think you're immortal.

When you see the subculture where drugs flourish you know that most of these people *are* buffoons. And they are not pleasant people. They're pigs, totally self-absorbed, totally self-destructive. Nothing is more important than getting the drug—except using the drug. If you knock over a junkie's spoon when he's cooking up, he'll kill you. And see it as justifiable homicide. If he bothers to think about it at all. Which he probably won't.

I got as far as doing heroin. Not for very long and not very heavily. Fortunately, it wasn't very easy to come by. The woman I was living with and I both did it. Then one day I came home and found out that she'd used up our entire stash. As I said, junkies get piggy. We weren't really junkies but we were certainly pigs. I was ready to kill her. Which gave me pause for thought.

I haven't taken drugs much since. Except for Jack Daniels and nicotine. Which of course aren't drugs but are really vital nutrients required by the human body.

When I left Reed for the last time, without getting a degree, I became a bartender. Laziness, once again. I though it was an easy job, not discovering until later you had to carry all those cases and kegs. And basically I'm a night person. Always had been—I remember wanting to stay up and watch Jack Paar as a kid, not ready to go to bed. I'd seen enough bartenders working to know it wasn't a bad job. It also struck me as very creative. You produced something.

And, of course, generally you don't need to have an alarm clock. You go to work in the afternoon, go to bed in the morning, sleep all day. But I liked the business primarily because it was creative—I even read books about it, the theory of making drinks. And I'd done a little bartending, back at the Playboy Club, filling in when somebody didn't show.

There's a kind of cameraderie among people in the business, and I like that. You hang out together and you go to each other's bars and leave fat tips. Actually, there should be some kind of bar money, like Monopoly money, designed just for that purpose—leaving tips—because the same cash just keeps moving around from bar to bar.

But I burned out on it after a couple of years. It's an exhausting lifestyle.

During all this time, the only opportunity I'd had to write came when some friends let me stay in their cabin for three months one winter. In exchange, I bought and helped them install some insulation. The cabin didn't have any electricity or running water. The water came from a logging flume behind the cabin, and when that froze up in the winter, I harvested icicles, like apples, and brought them in and cooked them down on the woodstove.

I was there with my two cats and my pregnant dog. After a month, she had fourteen puppies. She completely freaked out. Understandably. Fourteen little mouths lunging at her all day. I had to walk five miles to the nearest store to get powdered milk and pablum to feed the kids. I was fairly pleased, though, that my efforts as an adoptive mother paid off—only one of the puppies died, smothered beneath the rest.

So the cats and the dogs and I spent three months in this great cabin. I was writing short stories at the time.

I wrote a story about a guy who falls in love with a woman with no arms or legs. Back to severed limbs again—perhaps that's a pattern. Anyway, he kidnaps her and carts her around in a leather satchel. She's really the more adventurous of the two of them, and she's thrilled to be kidnapped. The relationship doesn't work out, unfortunately, because all her life she's dreamed about being rescued by some man who would love her despite the fact that she had no arms or legs, and now she's involved with a guy who loves her *because* she has no arms or legs. He points out that he loves her now for many more reasons, and that it shouldn't matter that he initially loved her for the wrong ones, but she doesn't buy that.

Weird stuff. More a bizarre kind of fable, really, than a short story. When you're living alone in a cabin for months, you start thinking weird. There are people who accuse me of never having recovered.

But it was the first uninterrupted time I'd ever had to write. It still hadn't occurred to me to try to write a novel. I didn't have the courage, maybe. Or maybe it was symptomatic of my being raised in this particular society, a consumer society. We're all programmed to consume, and producing something somehow seems foreign to us. So for a long time I wrote only short stories. I didn't know that the short story market was much tougher than the market for novels.

A year or two later, my grandfather died and left the kids, me and my brothers and sisters, a little money. This was sometime around the early seventies. I grabbed the cash and took off with my brother for Greece. We rented a house on an island called Karpathos, a beautiful, beautiful island, one of the few Greek islands that had huge stands of pine forest. Most of the trees had been stripped from Greece to make boats before Christ—Ancient Greek and Roman times. Then the goats ate the seedlings and that was it. Nothing left but bare rock.

I fell madly in love with this country. The light's like the light here in the Southwest, and the countryside is much like this one, except that there happens to be a nearby sea. The sea has always been important to me. My very earliest memory is being in water. And loving it. Cape May, New Jersey, when I was two years old.

So I fell madly, rapturously in love with this place, Greece. I don't know what I was writing then. I think it was a mystery novel. Yeah, the mystery novel format, a book set in the first half of the twentieth century, but it was really the Arthurian legend. The Pendragon Detective Agency run by Arthur, with a main character named Gowan, who was Gawain, who would never understand what the fuck was going on. It was full of anagrams and inside jokes. Inside medieval jokes, which as you know are hugely popular. The villain was Simon De Montfort, the head of the papal forces fighting the Albigensian Crusade against the heretics in the South of France. He would keep appearing as a different person. Morgan Le Fay showed up, too. It was a neat idea but totally impractical, or I just didn't have the talent or the patience to pull it off at the time. But that was the big plan.

I came back from Greece to Portland a year and a half later, met a

Greek woman, and mistook her for the country. Met her, fell in love with her—I was tending bar at the time in Portland—and I married her and we went back to Greece. The marriage didn't work out. It's hard enough to deal with a relationship when both members of it share at least a few similar cultural preconceptions. It's harder when they don't. When I left Greece, after a year and a half, I returned to New York, where I hadn't been since the late sixties, and got a job tending bar in New York. This was in 1976.

I went back to writing short stories. I had one whole wall lined with rejection slips. Then I wrote a letter to an editor—turned out she was the science editor—at *New York* magazine. I wrote her a query letter about an idea for an article talking about the bar business from the bartender's point of view. At the time, I was working at a terminally chic place called One Fifth in lower Manhattan. She said sure, let's talk, and we talked. It didn't actually work out, but she asked me if I had any other ideas, I said, yes, actually, I'd like to do a piece on psychics. I looked in the phone book under Psychic and there was a guy listed, a Dr. Steven Kaplan, who billed himself as the Director of the Vampire Research Association of America. So I talked with him and did the piece and *New York* published it. The first thing I'd ever had published. A hundred and fifty dollars. I remember getting the check. I went out to get a copy made before I cashed the original—my first check from writing. And, as I walked out, a bird shat on my head. It had to have been either a very large pigeon or a small condor. But I took it as a good omen. A favorable omen. I generally assume that all omens are favorable. It's probably not a safe assumption, but it's one that I can live with more comfortably.

I had been writing these sort of Nabokovian short stories, rich in language, I thought, but pretty short on plot—though not so bad as some of the minimalist stuff these days. Borgesian stuff as well. I was also reading a lot of mysteries at the time, as I always had been, and I'd been reading Jack Higgins, whose early books weren't all that great. I thought, well, shit, I can pull that off. So that's what I wrote. In my eyes it was at least as good as Jack Higgins' stuff. It was called *Cocaine Blues*, about a bartender who gets involved in a big drug deal in New York City. I'd never done any big drug deals, but I *was* a bartender and I knew the New York after-hours bar subculture pretty well. And those are the best parts of the book, I think. I sold that as a paperback original to Dell. Sold it as a proposal.

I took the advance money, quit my job as a bartender, and bought a share in a house on Ball Pond, Connecticut, with two other people. As it turned out, neither of them ever showed up, so I had the place to myself. I wrote the book in six months. Then I went to Greece to write another proposal. I wanted to write a book about Greece, wanted to do something that contained descriptions of the country, so I put together what turned out to be the proposal for a book called *The Aegean Affair.* While I was there in Greece, I heard about an island called Lamu, off the Kenya coast, and I decided that if Dell bought the proposal, I'd go there to write the book. Dell bought it, and I went to Africa to write a book about Greece.

I loved Lamu. It was great. The most beautiful place I'd ever seen in my life. The most magical. But initially I couldn't find a place to live. And then, once again, I lucked out. I was just about to leave Lamu and head down to Malindi, see if I could find a place there, when a man I'd met, Lars Korschen, helped me out. Lars and his family owned a hotel in Shella called Peponi, which in Swahili means either *cool* or *heaven,* which should tell you something about the climate. Lars called a friend of his, a man in Nairobi who'd been a member of the Polish Cavalry in World War II—the guys who charged German tanks on horseback—and asked him if I could rent his house for three months.

It was $350 a month, including a servant, and everyone told me not to give him any money or I'd spoil him. I did, naturally, being an American or liberal or whatever. Even so, I felt guilty for a while, at the notion of having a servant. But eventually, I confess, I got used to the idea. I used his first name later for the character in my African stories, Andrew.

He was a very nice guy, didn't speak a word of English and I didn't speak much Swahili. My character was something of an homage to him— to pay him back a little. Liberal guilt.

In order for me to work I have to structure my day. Make it almost prison-like. I get up, do my Zen sitting, my yoga, my calisthenics, eat breakfast, then I write for two or three hours. Sometimes, in the morning, I allow myself to read for a bit. In Kenya, before lunch, I'd go out spearfishing, get a fish, and Andrew would clean it for me, and then I'd cook it. In the afternoon, I write for two or three more hours, and then do dinner. In Kenya, at night, I had the option of putting on my Arab robe, so that I could feel like Lawrence of Arabia, and going down to the hotel, the Peponi, for coffee and Calvados. I'd sit on the the veranda and watch Arab dhows sail across the moon. It was great.

Then the advance money ran out and I had to come back to the States and go to work again. I hadn't finished the book, so I went to my mother's house in Florida for a while. I finished, sent it off, and then went to New Mexico, to Albuquerque, where my brother was living.

The two paperbacks were never reviewed, or at least I don't recall any reviews ever being sent to me by Dell. I *do* remember getting royalty statements that said "Unearned Income." A lovely phrase. What it means is that the book hasn't yet made back the advance. But I'd like to think it'd be possible for publishers to use some other expression. *Tax-free gift,* for example.

I got a new agent around that time and, between us, I didn't sell another book proposal for something like five years. I did write some short stories. My new agent told me, whatever you do, don't write about Africa. No one wants to read about Africa, she said. Well, I wanted to write about Africa, and since no one was buying anything I wrote, no matter what it was, I decided that I might as well write exactly what I wanted to.

The short stories *did* sell, but you can't make a living off short stories, and so for the next five years I was working as a bartender again.

I was living with my brother in Albuquerque, but I was dating a woman in Santa Fe and riding my motorcycle back and forth. Then someone offered me a housesitting job in Santa Fe. A *paid* housesitting job. I took it. I'd always liked Santa Fe, but I'd never been able to afford to live there. The housesitting thing gave me a chance to hang around a town I liked, and also to write a couple more of the short stories.

But eventually I had to take another job. Tending bar again. I also got another agent, Dominick Abel. I wrote a proposal using my Africa character, Andrew, and Dominick sold it to St. Martin's. So I took the money, which wasn't enough to go back to Kenya, and I went to Greece to write a book about Africa. Which struck me as nicely symmetrical, since I'd already done a book in Africa about Greece.

Then two things happened. It's much easier to do the background in a short story than it is in a novel, where you need a lot more depth and texture. By now, my memory of Africa had faded and I couldn't get a real handle on the country. I was having problems doing my research; I was living on an island called Kos and I'd go into Athens to try to find stuff about Africa and I couldn't find anything. And then that horrible famine hit, really awful pictures in the newspapers about starving kids. And there I am, trying to write a comedic mystery set in contemporary Africa. There was no way I could incorporate the famine, and no way I couldn't. I wrote to Dominick and said, "Look, this isn't going to work, I've spent the advance, what to you suggest?" He wrote back and said, "Give them another proposal and see if they OK it and we'll go on from there."

So I came back, wrote a proposal for a book called *Wall of Glass,* and St. Martin's liked it. I started tending bar *and* writing the book. I'd never done that before, worked full time and tried to write full time. It gave me a real appreciation for the people who can do it. It's real hard to have a life and write a book at the same time.

I outlined the Croft books in advance. When you're dealing with a PI, I think, you have to have something of a plan. The genre has been around a long time, and you've got to figure out ways to use the conventions and, in some cases, play against them. But I had no outline for *Lizzie* and no outline for *Wilde West,* which I think are better books than the first Croft novel.

Lizzie and *Wilde West* are what I call sport books, mutants. The ideas just came to me and since nobody had done quite the same thing, there wasn't any convention I had to follow. So I could just let the books take off.

EB: Since I've never been a person to let well enough alone, and since Walter Satterthwait, Silver-Tongued Devil, has just left his interviewer in the dust, I have to prod a little more, see if you're holding anything back. Don't you have any juicy biographical anecdotes which brilliantly illuminate the soul of your writing?

WS: I don't think so. We talked about the paradigm of the writer: being a night person, reading a lot, being solitary as a child, often coming from dysfunctional families (though everyone these days seems to fit that), so I don't think I have any more to say about myself, no.

EB: No choice little stories? Nothing about playing doctor, that sort of thing?

WS: I still like to play doctor from time to time.

EB: You seem to be guarding yourself rather well for the most part.

WS: All right, I do have a couple of stories about my father that I trot out from time to time. I'll give you one of the paradigmatic "My Father and Me" stories.

I had a baseball game coming up, an important game between my street and another, and my father decided I had to clean the garage that second, right then, couldn't be done later in the day. He told me he wanted the floor so clean he could eat off it. I was about twelve at the time. So I cleaned the garage and I did a good job. He came in and said something like, "That's not bad, but what's that pile of dirt in the center?" I said, "That's for you to eat."

So he said, "All right, go out in the woods and get me a stick for whipping."

Now this is one of those swell parental tricks I've since read about. Really abusive behavior, I think. George Bernard Shaw once said that the worst thing you could do is to beat a child in cold blood. But obviously it's not a swell idea to beat them in anger, either.

Anyway, he said, "Go to the woods and get a stick for me to whip you with." So I went into the woods and found a log, as heavy as I could drag back. It took me an hour to drag it back to the house. I rang the doorbell and said, "There's your stick," and then I ran.

Like Bob Dylan said, I ran away from home three times and they caught me every time but the last. I'd read a lot of survival books between ten and twelve and I knew a lot about the woods, and that was where I usually headed. I probably could have survived. Lived on berries and roots. An occasional antelope.

Anyway, that's the kind of relationship I had with my father. At a very young age I was taller than he was. He was built like a bull, but only about 5'7". I get the height from my mother's side of the family. My height didn't intimidate him, I don't think, but I know that it bugged him. He'd make me sit down when he bawled me out because he didn't like looking up at me, having me tower over him.

My father had never read my books. When he had a heart attack and they were doing a multiple by-pass, he had a stroke right in the operating room. He also had diabetes and they'd amputated some of his toes. Somebody had to go out and see him. First my sister did. Then I did. I hadn't seen him in twenty years. That's another story.

As I told you, I went to Greece for the first time with my brother. He'd left his money with my father and we'd gone over on my money. The idea was, when my money was gone, we'd send for his. Just as we were finishing up my cash, my brother got very sick, double pneumonia, and we needed his money, right away. I wrote to my father, asking for it. My father wrote back and said, "I won't send the money until Mark asks for it himself." Implying, of course, or so I felt, that I was going to steal it.

By then, fortunately, my brother had gotten better and we borrowed some money from a friend. I wrote back to my father a long and extremely unpleasant letter that told him essentially, and specifically, to go fuck himself. My brother talked me out of sending the letter, but I didn't speak to him again until he was dying.

I knew, going out there, that it would be the classic cliché. This big, burly, intimidating figure of my childhood would be a shriveled little thing lying in the hospital bed. And, sure enough, that's exactly the way it was. It was rough. And I hated it for being rough and also, maybe because I was a writer, for being such a stereotype of roughness.

EB: One question all writers have to get used to answering is the one about their literary influences (though this seems to border on insult, like "Who do you imitate and why?"): what books you loved, which writers really influence your life and writing, who you admire.

WS: By the time I was twelve, my mother had gotten a set of the Harvard Classics and I was reading out of that. I didn't read a lot of children's mysteries. I *do* remember reading a few of the Hardy Boys series and not particularly liking them. I liked Nancy Drew a little better. She seemed a bit less wimpy.

I got interested in Buddhism at eleven or twelve from the Harvard Classics. I also remember forcing myself through Shakespeare, although later, in college, I developed a huge crush on him. I suspect he may've been the Second Coming.

In high school I made up this program for myself which required that I read every important book ever written. I did pretty well, for an ignorant kid. More American and English stuff than, say, French. But I did read Flaubert and Zola and all of Stendahl. Stendahl knocked me out. Later, in *Wilde West,* I got a big kick out of playing around with his conception of love. I liked the Russians, too. Dostoyevski was terrific, and Tolstoy was maybe the Third Coming.

There was a time, fairly brief, that I read science fiction. I loved Roger Zelazny, especially *Lord of Light,* from which I also looted some stuff for *Wilde West.* Roger lives here in Santa Fe, and when I met him, I confessed the theft. And Robert Sheckley's short stories—extremely clever. I read some Asimov and some Heinlein, and enjoyed them both, particularly Heinlein.

But my interest always inclined more toward the hard-boiled mystery. Chandler, Hammett, Ross MacDonald. And Mickey Spillane. While he may not be a great writer, he's certainly not so awful as some people say he is. His early stuff is important, I think. Beneath the complacency of the Eisenhower years, there was a lot going on in this country. Rock and roll hit in the mid-fifties and it happened for a reason; we were looking for an outlet for some strong feelings. Spillane tapped into that.

I also remember picking up a copy of *Lolita,* which at the time was rumored to be a "dirty book." That book changed my life. That book showed me what you could really do with language. I didn't know at that point that Hammett and Chandler had been doing any more than telling a story. Reading Nabokov I realized that you could do more, that writing was more than storytelling. He was the guy who really showed me the craft—when I saw and recognized the play with language, the humor. Nabokov was the guy I really wanted to write like for many years after that, the guy I tried to write like, and I felt as though I'd passed beyond Hammett and Chandler. But, of course, they were no slouches themselves.

In high school I began reading Updike and Bellow and Mailer; I still like them all, even Mailer, although he seems to be traduced by everyone. He may be, or may've been, his own worst enemy, but over the years, I think, he's always tried to be honest. I've always had an enormous fondness and respect for him.

The big gaps in my English lit background are mostly nineteenth-century novelists, not a lot of whom I've read. I've never read Hardy or Trollope, for example. Nor very much Dickens, though I enjoy him very much when I read him. I thought *Bleak House* was terrific.

There are so many talented writers. That's probably why I started writing action-adventure: I didn't feel intimidated by the books. I didn't feel I had to be so good. Now I feel that I'm a pretty good writer. No Tolstoy, but pretty good. I like to think that each of my books has gotten better. And I'm especially proud of *Wilde West.* You don't sit down and decide to put dialogue into the mouth of Oscar Wilde unless you're overcome by a fit of hubris—and I think I did a pretty fair job of it. I bled over that book, although I hope it doesn't show. My blood, I mean; not the character's. The book does have, very visibly, a certain amount of character blood showing.

The stuff about the serial killer was extremely hard to do. Drawing stuff out of the back of your mind that you don't really want to know is there. I think it's in all of us, that darkness, but we don't want to know about it.

In a way, though, I'm fonder of *Lizzie* because it was the first time I took a stretch, and, because of the stretch, I was able to stretch Croft, my Santa Fe character, a little bit. I think going back and forth between the two kinds of books keeps me from getting stale, keeps me sharper. And, with any luck, it helps make each kind of book a little bit better.

EB: You are considered a Santa Fe writer, you actually use the place in your books. It has been my observation that they don't call New Mexico the Land of Enchantment for nothing. What hold does the Southwest have on you?

WS: Well, because I'd lived in Greece before I came here, I was already in love with the desert landscape. The space, the clarity of the light. And I like the multicultural atmosphere, which, fortunately, has gotten more multicultural and atmospheric. When I first arrived in Santa Fe, there were only a few blacks and almost no Orientals, and that's changed.

I love it here. The Land of Enchantment. A friend of mine calls it the Land of Entrapment. I like that. I remember telling another friend that I didn't like the landscape in the East as much because the earth is covered and you can't tell what it's thinking. I love the openness, the nakedness of the Southwest. The only thing I miss here is the sea. But the sea I can always go visit.

EB: By now you are a seasoned world traveler; you've been to Greece several times, Africa a couple, Thailand, and you're about to leave for Amsterdam. With all this gallivanting around the globe you're bound to have had adventures, stuff you can use in future books.

WS: Not really. I find a place to work and I get into my schedule, which involves a very structured day. I get up in the morning, do my exercises, have breakfast, work for two hours, go check my mail, come back, have lunch, work for two or three hours in the afternoon, make dinner, read for a while, and go to bed. That's it. There's no adventure there at all—I might as well be in Poughkeepsie as on a Greek island. The only thing I miss in Santa Fe is that I can't go spearfishing, the one sport I'm really good at. It's hard to incorporate spearfishing into the Santa Fe life-style.

EB: Not a lot of snorkeling in the Southwest this week?

WS: Apparently there's a lake over by Las Vegas, New Mexico, where spearfishing is allowed, but the water is extremely cold and I can't stay in cold water very long.

EB: Rudolfo Anaya has mythologized some lakes over by Santa Rosa, notably in his wonderful novel *Bless Me, Ultima.* You could go after the legendary giant goldfish that live in bottomless lakes there. But you express great love for both Africa and Greece so there must be things about those places that are special for you.

WS: The beauty, the scenery, and in Africa, the animals. It was a thrill to go into Tsavo game park and see a herd of elephants that hadn't been seen there in a long time. I expected them to be gray but these guys had been rolling in the mud and the mud was red. A herd of red elephants. It is incredibly beautiful country. I was also impressed by the baobab trees, the ones that look like they're upside down, like the roots are in the air. Legend has it that kings were buried in holes in the living trees and then sealed up.

EB: So they become part of the living tree? A curious kind of immortality.

WS: Right. I know it sounds romantic, Thailand and Africa and Greece, but I live exactly the same kind of life in each of those places. I just end up sitting in a room, writing a book. I go swimming. I get some exercise. Usually I'm working against a deadline so I've got to get started on the book and I can only come into town on the weekends and have drinks and coffee and then back to work and that's it. No excitement at all. It's really quite dull.

EB: Would you like to change that?

WS: No. I'm perfectly happy with that. This upcoming trip to Europe will actually be the first time I've played tourist; stopping at places and looking at things. Usually I'm in a hurry to get the work, the writing, done. This time I can take a bit of time off.

EB: So you were never chased through the streets by a pack of irate shoe-shine boys, never wandered into an opium den thinking it was a movie theater?

WS: No, I just find a house and I . . .

EB: Ate a sandwich you thought was ham on rye and it turned out to be roast elephant ear?

WS: If I found out it was elephant ear I probably would have been pleased. I don't have any problem with exotic food. I'll eat anything someone puts in front of me.

O. Henry Meets JACKTheRipper

L ike the phrase "kill for peace," the label "horror comics" is an oxymoron and has always seemed to me a misnomer. Oddly, though, there was a line of so-called comic books in the early fifties that had some success with this genre. The only title from the E-C Comics Group that survived the attacks of Dr. Frederick Wertham and his 1954 book *Seduction of the Innocent* was *Mad* magazine, which suggests the philosophical position of these offbeat comics. Like *Mad,* comic series like "Weird Fantasy," "The Vault of Horror," "Tales from the Crypt," and "Haunt of Fear" were marked by fearless antiestablishment humor and satire. E-C horror, science fiction, and war comics were full of tongue-in-cheek humor, absurd puns, and O. Henry plot twists. My favorite story was about an old couple who had fought for years. The old man finally decides he can't take another day of the old woman, so he kills her and buries her in the basement. Overheated from all that digging he takes some lemonade from the fridge, belts down a big glass, and is instantly struck down by enough poison to drop a football lineman. I also liked the one about the guy who falls in love with a pale, wan girl who seems to be a prisoner in her own house. He decides that her father, who dresses like Bela Lugosi and never leaves the house, is a vampire feeding on his own daughter, so he kills him. Turns out the girl was the vampire and she was weak from lack of fresh blood, which the young man provides.

Walter Satterthwait claims that his first and most devastating rejection came from E-C and remembers E-C comics fondly. Certainly there is a macabre thread that runs through Walter's own writing, and his taste in true crime runs to ax murderers and famous slashers. He has already used Lizzie Borden and Jack the Ripper in what I consider to be his two most original novels and both have scenes of graphic gore that imbed themselves in the reader's memory. At the same time I don't think anyone would accuse Satterthwait of lacking a sense of humor, avoiding irony, or eschewing the trick ending.

In the previously unpublished story "Lee Ann" we have all the ingredients for the classic E-C tale: graphic violence, disgusting characters, a grisly crime, a sarcastic voice, and a deliciously twisted ending. The dispassionate, calculated, cold-blooded narration propels the story which, reduced to a plot summary, is perhaps not all that original. It is the relationship of murderer and victim combined with the chilling voice of Jim Stoner that makes the story work for me. The humorous asides in the internal monologue make the character seem all the more horrific while at the same time removing the story a step or so from reality. About halfway through the reader stops taking the tale seriously and begins to anticipate the trick ending. Satterthwait, as author, realizes all this and designs an ending so novel and effective it will still be satisfying—still come as a pleasant surprise. Then, as a bonus, he adds a fillip at the very finish.

The story was rejected as too gruesome, but that charge only stands if the reader takes it too literally and fails to appreciate the tongue-in-cheek humor, the delicious details, the extra revelations in the denouement and the coda, which, like a Möbius ring, turns everything back on itself.

LeeAnn

And so I go in real quiet to check is everything okay. The lamp on the coffee table is on as per usual and the fire is lit in the woodstove we bought last winter. It's got a glass window in the front and inside there the flames are flapping like little arms back and forth.

I can hear the radio far off, so I know she's back in the bedroom listening to one of her dumb talk shows. As per usual.

I call out, "Hey, Lee Ann."

And she yells back in that scratchy whiny voice of hers, *"What?"*

"I'm home."

Nothing from her.

Hello Jim welcome home how you doing?

Yeah, sure.

I take off my jacket and lay it on the dinette table and I start pulling the stuff out of the pockets. I unfold the plastic poncho, it's thin and you can see through it, like Glad Wrap only thicker, and I slip it on. It's got these strings at the cuffs and I pull them tight. I get out the rubber gloves and I slip them on and make sure they're over the cuffs of the poncho. I bought the gloves and the poncho at K-Mart, different departments, different days. This was like three months ago.

I take out the knife. They call it a CIA letter opener. It's made of this amazing superstrong plastic so spies can carry it onto an airplane without getting caught, and it's real sharp, like a razor. You could shave with it, almost. I ordered it by mail from this place in California sells military stuff, and I had it sent to old man Mears's address, down the road. Old man Mears, he doesn't get home till after seven at night, and the mail comes by usually around four, so I just wait and check his box every day for three weeks until it comes. I paid for it, before, with a money order from the Seven-Eleven that I scribbled his name on. This was about three months ago also. I ordered two of them and I used one for practice. It worked fine.

We got one of these electronic cordless phones now in the kitchen. Lee Ann likes her gadgets, we got phones all over the place. We got a processor for food turns anything into a liquid, steak even. I pick up the phone and I walk around the corner to the living room where she can't hear me and I push the zero button for the operator.

The operator comes on and she says, "How may I help you." Very polite. I like that. Sometimes you get them, they're real snooty.

I tell her, "Please, miss, you gotta help me. I need an ambulance right away." My voice is all quakey and shakey.

"Is this an emergency, sir?" she says, and her voice is getting a little shakey also. I figure she's new at this. Well, me too. "Is this an emergency call?"

"Yes, please, you've gotta *help* me, she's lying here and there's blood all over, I don't know what to do." I should have been an actor, really.

"The address? What's the address, sir?" And I swear she makes a swallowing sound. New at this.

I give her the address, and I say, "You gotta *hurry*. The blood. It's awful. You *gotta*." I'm really falling apart now, is the idea.

"I will, sir, they'll be there as soon as they can," and by this time I swear she's almost crying. "I'm sorry. I'm sorry, sir, but I need your name."

"Jim Stoner," I tell her, and I hang up. She'll call the police up too, it's the law when someone wants an ambulance, police got to come along at the same time.

I go back into the kitchen, put the phone back on its recharger thing, and look at the clock on the wall. Ten thirty exactly. All systems go.

"Lee Ann," I holler.

No answer.

"*Lee Ann!*"

"*What,* for godsakes?" She's got a voice could cut through steel.

"Could you come out here a minute?" I call.

"I'm *busy,*" she hollers. Like nothing in the world is important except what *she's* doing.

"Lee Ann," I shout, "come on *out* here."

"What *is* it?"

"I gotta show you something. It's important."

Okay. Finally. Action. I hear her big feet slam against the floor when she swings herself out of bed, *timber,* and the *thump thump thump* as she comes marching up the hall in her socks. She always wears socks to bed, which I think is sort of a disgusting habit, personally.

I put the knife between my teeth like a pirate and I pull the plug from the microwave out of the wall, and then I pick the microwave up off the counter and I move back behind the door and hold it up over my head, and then soon as she comes through the door and starts looking around, saying, "*Well,*" in that nasty way she has, right then I smash it down on her head as hard as I can.

It's not as noisy as I thought it would be, and she hits the floor like a sack of potatoes. I dump the microwave, fling it away, and then I grab the cordless phone and get down on my knees next to her, real careful to tuck the poncho in under me so the blood won't get to my pants, and I turn her over, face up, and I start in on her with the knife.

They ever make a movie out of this, they should do this part in slow motion, with the knife rising and falling like it was underwater, because that's the way it happens, sort of. Up and down, up and down, slow and cloudy-like, with the blood spraying everywhere. I use the knife a lot because the idea I want to get across here, see, when they find her, is that it's some kind of crazy psycho person did this.

There's a lot of blood spreading across the floor, and I got to move her, tug her by her fat ankles across the linoleum, before it gets to my pants.

I stop for a while and turn on the cordless phone and dial Dr. Moore's phone number, which I committed to memory earlier. Dr. Moore comes on and I tell him, "Doctor, this is Jim Stoner and you gotta get over here right away! Sombody hurt Lee Ann!" I'm out of breath because of hauling Lee Ann around, so this sounds like genuine Oscar material here.

"Jim?" he says. "Jim Stoner?" Dr. Moore, he never was too swift on the uptake.

"You gotta get over here, Doctor! *Please!*" And I kind of gasp and I hang up.

I do a few more things with the knife, better safe than sorry, and then I quit. I stand up and look at the phone in my hand. No blood there, so I hook it back on the recharger.

The poncho is awful messy, like you might expect, so I slip it off me slow and easy and I put the knife inside there and fold the thing partway up. I strip off the gloves and stick them in the poncho and fold it up some more and I carry it over to the woodstove. I open up the stove door and shove the poncho in. Right away, *whoosh,* like I knew it would, it snaps up into flames, bright blue and yellow.

I close the door. The knife will go too. I tried this out with the first knife and it burned down to nothing in no time flat.

They could maybe find *something* in there, sure. I remember "Quincy." They got electronic stuff, lasers and all, can do wonders these days. But they got no way to prove it was me, see. Reasonable doubt. They got to prove it was me beyond a reasonable doubt. I rest my case, your honor.

I look around the room quick to see if I forgot anything. Looks good to me. Looks fine.

I go into the bathroom and check myself out in the mirror. Got a spot of blood, one tiny little spot, on my cheek. I rinse it off, run a towel over my face, and leave the water running in the sink to clean it out while I head back out to the kitchen.

Clock says ten thirty-seven, so seven minutes, which is pretty much what I figured, but it seems like a whole lot more time than that. That's why I say the slow motion thing if they do a movie.

Four months ago when this idea first came to me, I did an experiment where I called in and reported a fire at the Healeys' place, about two hundred yards down the road. Took the fire department and the state cops twenty minutes to get there, which meant the Healeys would have all been roast beef by then. Naturally I didn't use our phone to do the call. I used the one at the Seven-Eleven. My convenience store.

Okay. So I figure to myself I got at least another five minutes, conservative, before they show. I go into the bathroom and shut off the faucet, come back out and look around some more.

What about the door from the garage? Shouldn't it be open? I mean, I come in, I see Lee Ann lying there on the kitchen floor, and naturally I'm all horrified and everything, so wouldn't I leave the door hanging open and run over to her? I'm thinking this all out in my mind, see.

Cold outside. What I'll do, I'll tell them I left it open and then later I closed it because I was afraid the cold would get to Lee Ann. Naturally, the truth is that nothing at all could get to Lee Ann at this point in time.

Wait a minute, I think. Wouldn't I go over and check her out? Wouldn't I want to see if she was alive or not? Course I would. It's only natural.

So I walk over to Lee Ann. In order to reach her, I got to step in some of the stuff on the floor. Can't be helped, you take the bad with the good in this life. What I'd do if all this were real, I figure, is feel for her pulse. So I do. I pick up her fat arm and put my fingers against her wrist and hold them there . . . and *Holy God* it's not *possible,* not looking the way she does, not after all my *work,* but there it *is,* I can feel it move against the tips of my fingers real weak and slow and trembly like a tiny little wounded animal, but it's there, her pulse is there, and Holy God she's still *alive.*

I look around quick for something to bash her with, smash out that wicked little throb of life she's got, the *microwave,* a hammer, an ax, *anything,* but it's too late now, I can hear the siren, how'd they get here so damn *fast,* and I'm thinking, "Lee Ann if you ever loved me for one day in your whole fat rotten life do this for me now, please, please, please *die,*" and then their car is in the driveway and I'm running out to meet them.

*　　*　　*　　*

And so the cop says to me, "All right, Jim. Let's go over it one more time."

"I already *told* you everything, Lieutenant," I say. A hundred times at least. We been going round and round with this forever.

He nods. He's a big guy, they're all big guys, but he's wearing regular type clothes, a suit and tie and not a uniform like the others. He's maybe forty years old. We're in his office at the station in town.

"I know," he says. "Just one more time. When was it you last saw her?"

"Around six thirty."

"You left the house at six thirty?"

"I told you all this before."

"Where'd you go at six thirty, Jim?"

"Over to the mall. I met Jack Reuter there and we went to a movie."

"Which movie?"

"I told you. The Rambo movie. That Rambo Three."

"Good movie?"

"It was okay."

"What time did the movie start?"

"Quarter of eight."

"What time did it get out?"

"Quarter of ten, about."

"What'd you do then?"

"I hung around with Jack a while. And then I went home."

"What time was that?"

"Little after ten. Ten minutes after."

"How come Lee Ann didn't go to the movie?"

"She doesn't like movies. Lieutenant, can we call the hospital? Can we find out how she is?"

This is the hard part, see, trying to act like I'm all shook up about how Lee Ann is doing at the hospital. I *am* all shook up, sure, but not for exactly the reason I'm supposed to be.

It was weird, back at the house. Cops everywhere, and then the paramedic guys hooking tubes up to Lee Ann and carting her out to the ambulance like a bunch of Indians lugging a buffalo. I must have looked pretty nervous when they drove her away, because one of the cops puts his hand on my arm and he tells me, "Don't worry, Jim."

Yeah, I think. Easy for you to say. She can't send *you* to the Crisper.

But I discovered something about myself from doing what I did to Lee Ann. I discovered that even if I was nervous and worried, there was a part of me, way deep down, that I could move into and use as a hideout. It was kind of a place inside me that was strong, a fort, Fort Defiance, where no one could bother me, no one could hurt me. And so even if I wasn't too thrilled answering the same old questions again and again from the cops, I knew that no matter what happened I was going to be safe. I could escape when I wanted, at my ease.

So he says to me, the lieutenant, "They're doing everything they can, Jim. If there's any change they'll let us know. Now. You left the mall a little after ten."

"Right, yeah."

"You drove straight home?"

"Yeah."

"What time did you get there?"

"I told you," I tell him, "I don't know for sure. I didn't look at my watch. Ten thirty. I guess around ten thirty."

"Did you see anyone outside? Any cars parked along the road?"

"No."

He nods. "All right," he says. "You go inside. And then what?"

"Then I saw her *lying* there. Jeeze, do we got to *do* this again? I saw her lying there and for a minute I couldn't believe what I saw, and then I went over to her and I saw how bad she was hurt, and I was sick, and then I called up to get an ambulance."

"When did you call Dr. Moore?"

"A couple minutes later. The ambulance didn't get there right away, so I called him up."

"All right, now—"

A cop in uniform is knocking on the glass door of the lieutenant's office. The same cop who patted me on the arm back at the house. He's got one of those clipboards in his hand like a basketball coach and he's signaling with his finger for the lieutenant. The lieutenant gets up from behind his desk and tells me, "Hold on, Jim. Right back." And he goes outside and the two of them walk down the hallway out of sight.

I wonder is it about Lee Ann. *Lee Ann,* I think, *don't let me down now.*

I look around the lieutenant's office. On one wall there's a picture of the lieutenant and what I guess is his family. A gray-haired lady and a young kid and a girl wearing a high school jacket. Cute girl, blonde hair and blue eyes. Maybe I could get me something like that.

And it comes to me. Since Lee Ann's gone now, I can get me anything I want. I can do anything I want. I can do *anything* I want.

Except that Lee Ann's not gone, not yet . . .

I start getting nervous again, but then I slip down into my new center for a minute, maybe longer, down into my fort, and I get my strength together, they can't touch me, and then the lieutenant's coming back and I'm ready for him.

"Jim," he says, and he puts his hand on my shoulder. "I'm sorry. They lost her."

God bless you, Lee Ann. I got the strength now. Goddamn, I got the strength and I can do anything. I let my shoulders go loose and I lower my head and I put my hand up to it.

He sits on the edge of the desk and I can feel him looking down at me, I can feel his eyes through the bones of my hand. "It was just too much," he tells me. "What happened to her."

I nod into my hand. Laurence Olivier we're talking here.

"Jim," he says.

I look up and the amazing thing is I'm really crying. I can feel the tears moving down my face like little snails. From relief, I figure.

"Jim," he says. "It's never easy. I'm sorry we had to put you through it. But we had to make sure." He takes a big deep breath. "That's our job, Jim. We have to look into everything. And we did. And your story checks out. I just want—"

There's another knock on the glass door and I look up and a new cop is standing out there, no clipboard. This one uses his whole hand, not just his finger, to signal the lieutenant. The lieutenant says, "Hold on, Jim," and he pats me on the shoulder again and he goes outside. They like patting you on the shoulder, cops.

I think for a second that maybe Lee Ann, maybe she's come back from the dead, be just like her to rain on my parade, but then I figure that's crazy. Not even Lee Ann could pull that off.

So I'm staring at the picture of the lieutenant's daughter when he comes back in, and what I'm doing, I'm mapping out all these new freedoms I got. Wine and women and song. It's all there for me now.

Two other guys come in with the lieutenant, the cop he left with and another guy, little guy in a raincoat with fidgety eyes. The lieutenant, he's carrying a tape recorder.

He says to me, and there's something strange in the way he talks, "I think you better listen to this, Jim." And then he sets the machine on his desk and he hits one of the buttons with his finger. His hand is shaking now like he's got a bad case of flu.

"*Hello, caller?*" the machine says. "*Are you there?*"

"*Hello?*" It's Lee Ann's whiny voice, which I never thought I'd ever hear again, naturally. "*Dr. Bob?*" I get this prickly feeling on my skin, like the hair there is starting to grow backwards, towards the bone.

Machine says, "*Go ahead, caller, you're on the air. What's your name?*"

"*Lee Ann.*"

"*How are you tonight, Lee Ann?*"

"*Okay I guess.*"

"*And what would you like to share with us, Lee Ann?*"

And Lee Ann, I can't believe this, Lee Ann starts whining and moaning about *us*, about *me*, telling the whole world what a terrible hard time she's having with *me*. Blaming *me* for everything, as per usual.

The lieutenant nods to the little guy and says to me, "This is Dr. Freeman," and his voice rides higher over Lee Ann's creepy whining. "He's a psychologist. He's got a call-in program here in town. He was still down at the radio station when he heard about Lee Ann's death, and he brought us the tape."

He turns to the little guy. "What time was the tape made, Doctor?"

"What?" The little guy can't take his weaselly eyes off of me, it's like he's hypnotized. "Oh. She called at twenty after ten tonight."

"I can't ask him to do anything, Dr. Bob," says the mechanical Lee Ann. *"He won't help me do anything around the house at all."*

The lieutenant's smiling a funny smile. "This is the part, coming up," he says. "Listen to it, Jim."

Lee Ann complains some more, and then—

"Hey, Lee Ann." I recognize my own voice even though it's small and all muffled up like it's coming through cloth.

"What?" she hollers back, and then she's whispering, louder than her holler, hissing like a snake from the machine, *"That's him, Dr. Bob, that's Jimmy. I gotta go."* And then I hear, *click.*

The lieutenant pushes the button on the tape machine and he crosses his arms and stands there looking down at me.

They're all looking down at me, leaning the weight of their eyes on me, all three of them standing there in that white florescent light that makes dark shadows like black paint on their faces.

The machine's off now, but I can still hear Lee Ann whining . . . *"I know I'm only his stepmother and all but listen, Dr. Bob, since his crazy father died I been father and mother both to him, and I swear he's gonna be the death of me."*

And the lieutenant says, "You're through, kid. You're history."

And I smile up at him and a part of me slips back into my center, my core, where they can never get to me, never touch me, never come close in a million years. And the light gets whiter all of a sudden and their faces get strange, the paint is darker, the paint is blacker, and colors are curling at the edge of the picture, brown and red and orange like it's starting to burn, like there's a fire hungry behind it and the fire's going to eat it all away. And then suddenly it does, a bright flame bursts blue and yellow across everything, *whoosh,* and then it's gone, it's gone, everything is gone.

Gone.

Everything is.

Okay. Everything is okay. Everything is okay.

And so I go in real quiet to check is everything okay. The lamp on the coffee table is on as per usual and the fire is lit in the woodstove we bought last winter. It's got a glass window in the front and inside there the flames are flapping like little arms back and forth. . . .

The Interview

EB: I know you counter the stupid question, Where do you get your ideas from? by saying you've got an old guy in Ohio who sends them to you in the mail. All the same, where did *Wall of Glass* come from?

WS: It probably isn't as good a piece of writing as some of the African stories. It began as a sort of a gimmicky Nero Wolfe–ish thing, where one of the characters wouldn't be leaving the house for some reason and the other would be out doing the legwork. Croft would be smart, but not so smart as Rita.

EB: Actually, I spotted her as a Nero Wolfe character at first glance but then you tricked me by not using her that way. Hardly using her at all, as a matter of fact, though you may want to refute that.

WS: I suppose I could write a Joshua Croft novel without her. But I like her. The problem is—how do I bring her more into the story when she's paralyzed? I discovered, after I started writing the book, that I didn't want her to be in a British-style puzzle mystery—after all, these are American private eyes.

In the next book, *A Flower in the Desert,* as a matter of of fact, she's a good deal more involved in the story. And from now on, she'll be more active. In *At Ease with the Dead* her paralysis was beginning to improve.

In the next book she'll be up and about. She'll be working on a case of her own, using a computer to untangle some piece of financial chicanery I haven't decided on yet. Her case will unfold as she tells it to Joshua, and his case will unfold as he tells it to the reader, and both cases will be solved at the same time. Rita will comment on that, probably. She likes to comment on things.

EB: You wanted her out of the wheelchair.

WS: I wanted her out of the wheelchair, yeah. And, when I've done signings, a lot of people have asked when I'm going to get her out. This is one of the longest cases of coitus interruptus on record. Longer than Tristram Shandy's parents'.

EB: How self-consciously did you attack *Wall of Glass* when you finally decided to do a mystery? It has a lot of the formula bits, after all. Sticks to the conventions of the genre down to the friend on the police force that all detectives seem to have to have.

WS: Yeah, Hector Mendoza. It seemed to me that I had to have that character. I'd talked to an investigator when I first started, and he told me you'd almost have to have a friend in that position. I talked to some cops, too. Let me say that cops—despite the thugs who screwed up in Los Angeles, the ones who beat Rodney King—I generally admire cops. I think they have the roughest job there is. They're underpaid and frequently they're destroyed by their work: alcohol, divorce, eventually seeing the world as filled with maggots, and not being able to stop the maggots because things—like the courts and the laws and sometimes the civilians—get in the way. It's a really nasty job, and I never wanted to say anything about it that wasn't true. So I talked to cops.

And still do. For the new book I talked recently with a really pleasant woman at the New Mexico State Police. I wanted to know what state police investigators (state cops other than highway patrol) were called— it's *agents,* by the way. I wanted to know where they had jurisdiction and where they could be sent. These agents investigate crimes in places where the local sheriff's office just isn't up to it. And they handle forensics for almost everybody in the state.

EB: How do you pursue a question when it comes up?

WS: That's part of the fun of it. You find out how you find these things out. You learn how to learn. The author as detective. If I have a question about cops, I call the cops. The premise of the new book is that Croft is hired by a public defender. So I called a lawyer who sometimes works as a public defender and asked her how she might go about hiring a PI.

EB: Back to the formula. You outline the Croft novels before you begin so you know where you were going with them. You know the stock elements.

WS: They're stock because they have some approach to reality. Clichés are clichés for a reason. No PI could operate without some contact on the police force.

EB: How conscious are you of the conventions that must be followed, such as introducing the villain early in the book?

WS: You have to play fair, it seems to me. You don't trot out the villain at the end of the book, someone who hasn't been seen before.

EB: You have to keep all those things in mind and still write a good story. I don't suppose anyone would write a mystery without

Photo by Ernie Bulow

keeping those conventions in mind, it would never get published—but the question is how conscious are you of them, are you inclined to push the boundaries of the genre and do you feel particularly restricted by the traditional requirements? How do you make a mystery novel your own?

WS: When I began the book *Wall of Glass,* I don't think that I consciously sat down and thought, well . . . you have to put the villain up front, you have to do this, you have to do that. I've read mysteries and private-eye novels for most of my life, and, subconsciously, I suppose, I've assimilated the conventions.

The later books play around with the conventions a bit. In *Wilde West,* there's a character who doesn't show up until quite late. I put him in late deliberately, because I wanted to see how that worked. I think it worked out okay.

I think, too, that *At Ease with the Dead* is a more ambitious book than the first Croft novel.

EB: It feels looser to me, looser in a positive sense. Less formulaic. That's why I asked the question, because I remember first reading *Wall of Glass* and being pretty aware of your use of the conventions: Joshua Croft is a smartass, he swims laps and plays racquetball, has a friend on the police force, you kill off a guy in the first chapter, your hero doesn't carry a gun, the cops warn him off the case—an insurance claim thing—while each chapter ends with some device like a gunshot. In other words, everything was in the right place.

WS: There's a great Chandler line, something to the effect that when things get a little dull, you can always have a guy come in with a gun and start shooting. I found that I'd reach Chapter Seven or Eight, and I sensed that nothing very exciting was happening, there was no real action going on. So let's do something, I decided. And I threw a fight in between Croft and what's-his-name, Killebrew. But I don't know if there was a conscious awareness that I was following conventions. I mean, I like these books and I guess I like the conventions. Fights are fun. In a book, anyway.

Wall of Glass was not all that conscious a book, in spite of the fact that I'd outlined it, just as I subsequently outlined the next Croft books.

EB: That's interesting, because it reads, just marginally, stiffer. *At Ease with the Dead,* until the shootout at the end, is far less predictable, let's say.

WS: Part of the reality of that book, the writing of it, was that I could only get to it, actually sit down and plug away at it, for two or three days a week. I was working full time as a bartender. And also, I wasn't sure at the time if this was the way I wanted to go with my writing. And then I started to like the characters. Joshua, Rita. Really started enjoying them. And then, I think, the book kind of took off.

But then, toward the end of it, I had the idea for something involving Lizzie Borden. Wanted to do it right away, and not do a *Wall of Glass* sequel. My agent felt that St. Martin's would prefer a sequel, so I suggested to him—or he suggested to me, I forget now—that I do a couple of chapters of the Lizzie Borden thing, and also an outline for a new Croft book, and see whether St. Martin's would spring for a two-book contract. I did that, and St. Martins, bless them, went along.

Anyway, *Wall of Glass* was a first mystery, and I think it shows.

EB: Not that that's a criticism necessarily. What I'm fishing for is where these things come from, what all writers do alike and what they do differently.

WS: I don't know where they come from, actually. The little old guy in Ohio. The unconscious. The ether. All of which are probably the same thing. They come from everything you've ever read or seen or heard. I have what's probably an irrational fear that if I try to analyze where these ideas come from, they won't come from there anymore. You just accept them when they come, and you accept, on faith, that they're going to keep coming. But if you ask me why I did *that* kind of mystery, it's because I've always liked *that* kind of mystery, with the private detective who's a kind of wiseass and who solves the case and finds out what's going on. The formula. But a sonnet is a formula, too, and you can do all kinds of things with a sonnet. I didn't do as many things as I probably could have done, but I think that. . . .

EB: I'm leading you on here because I have some definite ideas about the subject myself, of course. Ultimately, I think your strength, your literary achievement will be in the way you push the genre, as seen in *Miss Lizzie* and *Wilde West,* which are both excitingly different sorts of books.

I've always been opposed to the idea of the formula because I think it is misleading and uninformative. I wrote a paper once, many years ago, that I read at a popular culture meeting in Indianapolis, and it pissed everybody off because I took on Max Brand, who is supposedly *the* formula western writer, and insisted that, contrary to the formula theory, the things that made him readable and popular and enduring were the same things that make literature literature: good plotting, solid character development, and so on. In a bizarre way, he was antiformula. It didn't go over well. I think people like their formula writers to be formula writers. But I don't think an analysis of the formula tells you much. It's too simplistic. Like trying to explain the popularity of a Cadillac in terms of how many pounds of iron it takes to build one.

WS: No, formula analysis doesn't tell you much. In *Wall of Glass,* as in most contemporary mysteries, there's an awareness of the tradition. Inevitably, the tradition is being commented upon. At one point, one of the characters mentions *The Rockford Files.* A friend on Paros, where I wrote *Wilde West,* read *Wall of Glass* and *Miss Lizzie,* and he liked *Wall of Glass* better, because he saw it as postmodern, whatever that means. Whereas, for him, *Lizzie* is traditional. Whatever that means. I suppose what he's saying is that in the PI books, there's an awareness on the part of the characters that they work within a tradition—two traditions, one real, the other literary. There's a history of mystery writing, and of private detective mystery writing, and of film and television detective mystery writing, so these people are operating in a world that's aware of the world in which they find themselves live.

But that's true, too, of real PI's in the real world. Whatever that is.

EB: In a way you had a double problem in *Wall of Glass,* because you had all those conventions of the mystery hanging over you, as every mystery writer does, and you had the Santa Fe mystique hanging over you too. As cities go, Santa Fe is almost formulaic. Beyond its Hispanic and Indian underpinning, it is the only city I know of that has been consciously crafted by the artists and writers who have lived there for the last hundred years. They have city ordinances that keep all the buildings looking the same. So-called Santa Fe style has become a cliché. Yet underneath that there is a romance and originality, a soul, that is unique.

WS: Croft doesn't buy it entirely.

EB: But you don't exactly debunk the Santa Fe myth.

WS: But he's amused by that aspect of Santa Fe life. Art galleries, cowboy glitz . . . I went to an art opening last night, for the first time in a long while, and I thought, good Lord, here I am, Joshua Croft at an art opening, listening to the conversations. You don't have to parody a lot of the people who show up at an art gallery opening. They do it for you.

EB: You didn't feel like you had to go to a particular opening to write it into the book.

WS: No, no. Not a specific gallery opening. You know, I've been to art openings and I've heard the most bizarre things being said with an absolutely straight face. And it was fun, I enjoyed it. I suppose that's what I was trying to get over with Croft, amusement without any real contempt.

EB: It works pretty well, but you forgot to work in some cactus and a couple of coyotes. I can't think of any other place as distinctive, not even

San Francisco or New Orleans. I'm glad you don't have to call it by some made-up name, like Grafton refers to Santa Barbara as Santa Teresa.

WS: Yeah, and Chandler called Santa Monica something else. Bay City, if I remember correctly.

EB: I'm glad that convention is long gone.

WS: I don't know why Grafton did it.

EB: But you still avoid using real gallery names, and I noticed in the short story "A Matter of Pride" you made up fictitious names for bars.

WS: Yeah, any scenes set in a gallery are not set in a real gallery, although I mentioned real restaurants and bars in the novel. I mentioned Vanessie's, where I used to work. But no, I didn't use real names, not with the galleries. If I'm setting a scene in a house, usually I won't specify where the house is located, because somebody will come tell me later, "You're talking about my house and I don't like it."

EB: I've wondered about that, about how much one can get away with. John Dunning, from Denver, just wrote a book that's pretty much a roman à clef. Dunning was pretty blatant with his use of local booksellers and stores, all of which are obvious to anyone who knows the local book scene, and even the villain is a real person, who *knows* that he's been used, and is flattered because he doesn't know that he's not supposed to be.

WS: I never use any real people. Maybe a gesture, or a characteristic, of someone I know.

EB: Of course, inevitably that's another of those questions that always comes up. How autobiographical? I pop up in a chapter of Ed Abbey's book *A Fool's Progress,* so I know exactly how much he fictionalized that part. Actually, it was quite a lot. He still drew on a real person, a real situation, real relationship. I think that of all the writers that I know, and know how they work, the ones that are the best, the most fun to read, who manage a steady output of quality material, are the ones that are out there having a lot of experiences, who are doing things, who have a lot of friends, who listen to people in conversation. You have to have something to draw on. I think there aren't very many writers who can fabricate and I think eventually you get tired of them. Like John Irving. He works so symbolically; using bears, raped women, hotels, zoos, wrestling, Vienna, etc., etc. His books may be brilliantly written, rather cerebral, but ultimately repetitious and disappointing. I can think of other novelists who are so removed from what's happening, so out of touch with regular people, that they simply don't write anymore.

WS: I limit how far I'll go with real life. There's no one character in any of my books to whom anyone can point and say "That person is so-and-so." I don't use real people. Forgetting the unpleasant possibility of a libel suit, there's also the fact that if you use a real live person, you infringe upon their privacy, and I don't think that's a fair thing to do. Whether I've got five thousand, ten thousand, fifty thousand or some day, maybe,

if I'm lucky, a hundred thousand readers; it's not fair that they know something about a person who has a real life. No matter how obnoxious I might find that particular person, it's not fair to put them up to public scrutiny. Unless they're doing something that I feel is dangerous, in which case, probably, I wouldn't use fiction to talk about it.

EB: But of course your readers would never know how close a character was to a real person, unless they were in your immediate

Photo by Ernie Bulow

circle. Only a few people knew I was the model for the Abbey character. I suppose that doesn't count for really public people that have given up their rights. You can make fun of the president if you want.

WS: Which of course is shooting fish in a barrel. In the new book, the New Age healing book, there will be people who'll bear a certain resemblance to actual people floating around Santa Fe. But the characters in the book *won't* be the real people. For legal reasons as much as any other. The only thing the real people might have in common with the characters will be obnoxiousness, and that would be a very poor argument to bring to court.

EB: There are a lot of New Age people in Santa Fe. They're ubiquitous.

WS: Something for everyone. I told you about hair balancing?

EB: No.

WS: Hair balancing is a technique whereby the guy cuts your hair in such a way that it balances the electromagnetic field of your body. Whenever I hear about hair balancing, I always think of Curly, one of the Three Stooges. Infant massage is another one I like. It's supposed to produce more peaceful kids. And you've got to figure that at least it can't take very long, because, after all, infants have those tiny little bodies. So even if it's expensive, it won't take much time out of your infant's busy schedule.

EB: That's one of the curious things about a place like Santa Fe. Whatever its harmonic convergence is, it collects strange people.

WS: It's amazing. You look at the bulletin board in the library, the posters and flyers, and the variety of this shit is actually astounding.

EB: Remember the rubber lady?

WS: Sure. I never knew who she was, but I knew people who did.

EB: I never met her, but she used to advertise for parties and things. I never did exactly find out what her schtick was.

WS: She came all dressed in latex, black latex. Her face was covered. She'd show up at different events, particularly when the Ugly Building went up downtown, the First National Bank building. She showed up a lot, and, like I say, I don't know who she was, but I think it's neat that there's someone in this town who *was* the rubber lady, and who's walking around with that awareness.

EB: We know it wasn't you, because the rubber lady wasn't 6'4". Actually, you took it kind of easy in *Wall of Glass* compared to what you might have done. There's so much really nutty stuff going on here all the time that you could have been much wilder.

WS: No, it's not bad at all. I've never dealt with the real underbelly, the hidden undercurrents, of Santa Fe.

EB: John Nichols would tell you that would be your obligation. That's almost a crusade of his, that the old Hispanic families have been driven out, not only in the economic sense but in the literal sense, that the land value is getting so high, the taxes and what not, that families who have owned land here for more than four hundred years have to give it up because it's worth too much. I know a family in Gallup with a grandmother who's hanging on to a piece of land up here and the whole family has to help her with the property taxes; the taxes are becoming prohibitive. The house really isn't worth that much, she's an old lady, but they keep reassessing it and . . . that is a reality. The old Hispanic families are relegated mainly to service occupations.

WS: I've touched on the plight of the Hispanics. There's Norman Montoya in *Wall of Glass,* and he shows up again in the new book, *A Flower in the Desert.* And I mention that the early Hispanic settlers' land was essentially stolen from them by the federal government. So I suppose that my liberal credentials are pretty much intact.

And there are still many aspects of Santa Fe that I haven't dealt with, and that could provide more background for my future books.

EB: You could play with the stuff going on at Los Alamos, the mysterious space-age pollution.

WS: Sure. There are a lot of things. I'm not going to exhaust Santa Fe. I like it, and for the first time I'm doing two Croft books in a row, and I'm excited about the next one because I'm playing around with the plot by using the Tarot deck as the structure. And I like the book I just finished, *A Flower in the Desert.* That one has to do with El Salvador and with sexual child abuse, and, to my way of thinking, there are certain thematic similarities between the two. Other people may not agree, and some people may be thoroughly pissed off that I think so.

EB: Didn't Abraham Lincoln say, "You can't please all the people all the time"?

WS: There are people who love the Croft books, who like *Miss Lizzie,* but who can't stand *Wilde West.* There are people who love *Wilde West,* think the Croft books are OK, think *Lizzie*'s pretty good. There are people who are really pissed off that I don't do Joshua Croft books all the time. Whenever I do a signing, I'm always surprised by the variety of reactions to the books.

EB: As we were saying, it pushes you forward in the craft, keeps you fresh, and all those things. I think it's a great idea and I think more writers are beginning to do things like alternate between series and nonseries books so they don't get stale. You said earlier you had the idea for *Miss Lizzie* before you had finished the first Croft book. What made you think of that book?

WS: Lizzie Borden had fascinated me from the time I was a kid. In fact, the first true crime book I ever read was a book by Edward Radin called *Lizzie Borden: The Untold Story*. Obviously, the idea of patricide, matricide, is fascinating to a kid, and Lizzie, if she was guilty, actually got away with it. I think I've probably read everything ever written about her. I originally thought about using her in a short story for *Alfred Hitchcock's Mystery Magazine,* with which I'd established a nice relationship because of the African stories. So I thought that I'd take time off between the two Croft books and do a short story for them. Initially, the idea was I'd have a young boy who lived next door to Lizzie and who somehow became involved with her. And then I thought, hell, there's a lot of stuff written about Lizzie Borden, and I could play around with some of that. It would take more than a short story to do her justice. And there was other stuff I wanted to do—for example, I wanted to use Hammett's Continental Op.

EB: Where did that connection come from?

WS: I'd been reading a biography of Hammett. Anyway, the project was already turning into a book. And then, after I started, it occurred to me that a young girl would make a better protagonist. She'd be able to get closer to Lizzie. With a young girl, I thought, Lizzie would be much more likely to let down her hair, and I wanted her to let down her hair. I wanted her to reveal more of herself.

So then, I thought, Jesus, can I pull this off, can I create a persuasive woman narrator? I'd never tried that. But finally I decided that I could do it. Amanda, the narrator, appears only as an eighty-year-old woman or a thirteen-year-old girl. I eliminated the entire middle portion of her life, where I would've had to do things like passion, love, marriage, sex. So in a way, like a lot of writing, it's sleight of hand. And, too, in 1921 and perhaps even now, young boys and girls of twelve or thirteen were much more alike than they were different, I felt, and it seemed to me that I could draw upon what I remembered of my own adolescence.

I liked the idea that the eyes of the main character don't see every-thing, can't see everything, and that the mind behind the eyes doesn't understand a lot of what's going on. She certainly doesn't understand her crazy mother, nor the remoteness of her father. I thought I handled the parents nicely. Anyway, there was way too much stuff for a short story.

EB: You said you think you've read everything ever written about the Borden case so your handling of her was presumably based on reality. What surprised me most as I got into the novel was how little I knew of the historical case. All I knew about Lizzie Borden was that she was a girl who supposedly offed both her parents with an ax. Pretty horrid, heinous crime, especially in those days.

WS: She wasn't really a girl. She was thirty years old at the time of the murders. I assumed, before I first read anything about her, that she was younger, too.

EB: My question is, as an artist, a writer, did you actually use too little of that material?

WS: I think I used enough for what I wanted to do.

EB: Here I am, the analytical reader, overeducated critic, saying, "Oh no, we're gonna get the whole Lizzie Borden case," and then in the end I was disappointed because I didn't get enough of it.

WS: All you hear about the original murders is what you hear from the young boy, the one Amanda has a crush on.

EB: I was afraid you would overdo it, give us too much of the original story. By the end I wished you had given us more, especially on the subject of her apparent guilt. You've got your own theories, obviously, and you never share them.

WS: It seems to me there are already enough books about the murder. Anyone who's really interested in the murder of Lizzie's parents can find books about it. I wanted to put in enough stuff for the people who didn't know, to enable them to know what the original story was.

EB: You've raised what I consider a knotty philosophical question. Here's a woman that we admire—we like her, but if she committed the murders and we still like her, then we've got a philosophical position where we need to justify the crime, except you don't ever bother.

WS: It's interesting, though, to be put in that position, don't you think?

EB: It's interesting but it's nerve wracking too. It reminds me of a cello piece someone played for me once where the composer keeps refusing to resolve the chord, complete the harmonic progression, and by the end of the piece the listener's nerves are pretty raw. You are definitely looking for the resolution.

WS: That's not necessarily the response. My theory on Lizzie Borden is that the maternal link was nonexistent. Lizzie never liked her stepmother. As for her father . . . there's no way to prove it now, obviously, but I suspect that she was abused by him. Sexually.

And, according to Veronica Lincoln, who wrote what I think is the best book on the Borden killings, Lizzie probably had frontal lobe epilepsy. That's a condition in which, apparently, you can act violently and, afterward, be totally unaware of it.

You have to see the Borden house, on that day in August, in perspective. First, it was the hottest day of the year. Sweltering.

Photo by Ernie Bulow

Next, there was, there had been for a long time, this terrible animosity between Lizzie and her stepmother. Lizzie was having her period, which, according to Ms. Lincoln, made her more prone to the epileptic attacks. It's entirely conceivable to me that something was said, or done, by the stepmother, and, in a fit of anger, a fury of anger, Lizzie just went wacko and hacked her stepmother to death. Then her father came home early. Ms. Lincoln believes, and I'm inclined to agree with her, that if LIzzie had just killed her mother, she *had* to kill her father—so that he wouldn't know what she'd just done. If she did kill her father, she killed him to spare him that knowledge, and to spare herself his horror at the knowledge. She loved her father. There was an enormously strong bond between them.

EB: It appears that it was probably perverted.

WS: From what I've read, sexually abused children often appear to be fonder of the parent who abuses them sexually. So, if in fact she did have this attack of frontal lobe epilepsy, was she perhaps less culpable? Assuming she did kill them, does that mean that forever afterward she's irredeemable? And maybe she didn't kill them. Whether she did or not, who knows what agony she might have gone through?

EB: Virtual isolation all those years.

WS: She says at some point that we create our own hell.

EB: Why was the real Lizzie Borden acquitted?

WS: Partially, as someone once said, because the prosecution never got a fair trial. They weren't allowed to introduce her inquest testimony, which clearly contradicted some of the statements she made during the trial. Partially because no one wanted to believe that an upper-middle-class woman could do such a thing.

EB: Obviously Amanda doesn't have any problem with her friend's past.

She's a great narrator and a strong character, and she adds a lot to the book.

WS: It's a book I'm real fond of. It was an easy book to write. I would just sit at the computer and assume this sort of mantle, the Mantle of Amanda, and, in a weird way, Amanda would write the book herself. I wrote it in drag, in a sense.

EB: That is interesting, because I would think that maintaining that voice in a credible way would be very hard.

WS: I had to go back, often, because once in a while I'd slip in a contemporary word or idiom. When I finished, I went back over the whole and took out all the contractions. But basically it was an easy book to write.

EB: The Oscar Wilde book was more difficult?

WS: Of course, primarily because of the difficulty of writing dialogue for a character as witty as Wilde, that took a lot of nerve, and also because I was using third person. All my other books are in first person. And *Wilde West* has multiple points of view, jumping from the viewpoint of one character in one chapter to the viewpoint of another in the next.

EB: Why use Oscar Wilde at all?

WS: Originally, I wanted to do a book that had Oscar Wilde solving the Jack the Ripper killings. Because the Ripper killings were, again, something that I'd read a lot about. There's a huge, huge literature on the subject.

EB: It's been used a number of times in novels. *The Lodger* is a genre cornerstone.

WS: Sure, but not with Oscar Wilde. But, the year I submitted the proposal to St. Martin's happened to be the centenary of the Ripper killings, and there were sixteen or seventeen books about Jack the Ripper coming out. Tom Dunne, at St. Martin's, thought, and probably correctly, that my book would've gotten lost in the shuffle. My agent, Dominick Abel, suggested that I stick with Oscar Wilde. He liked the idea.

I knew that Wilde had done a tour of America, and it occurred to me that it might be fun to put Wilde down in the American West and have him solve what are, in effect, Jack the Ripper killings, or at least have him investigate them in some capacity. And then, actually, I'd have something a little more interesting to work with. You've got this aesthetic, dandified Englishman in the middle of miners and cowboys and ranchers, lumber and silver barons. It seemed to me that there were a lot of comic possibilities there. Misunderstandings, cross-cultural conflicts. And I think that it came out a better book than the Ripper book would've been.

It's hard to be fond of a book in which there's some really rough stuff, and *Wilde West* does have some pretty rough stuff in it. Probably I'm not fond of it in the same way I'm fond of *Miss Lizzie*. But I'm proud of this book and I think I did pull it off.

I can understand, on the other hand, why some people haven't liked it. It's different from the other books, and many people can't enjoy a book that has heinous crimes, graphically described. That's fine, I understand that. But I'll argue to my dying day that it's basically a comedy. That's the way I see it. I get a big kick out of Oscar himself.

EB: I was fascinated with him too at one time and I read a lot about him and I read most of his major works, especially loving *The Picture of Dorian Grey*. His plays are wonderful for their use of language. I've always been very impressed with someone that can handle language like him. He would probably love Fletch and the wiseass detectives. I'm sure he'd approve of the lines you gave him.

WS: What impressed most people at that time was this amazing ability to extemporize, to fabricate on the spur of the moment complete stories that were coherent, witty, insightful. Evidently, the people who knew him were more engaged by him as a personality and as a raconteur than they were by his writing.

EB: I know something of the sensational morality trial. In your story he had apparently not changed sexual preferences yet.

WS: Well, according to Richard Ellman's biography, which by the way is a terrific piece of work, up until the time Wilde was married he'd never had an active homosexual relationship. That didn't happen until after he was married and had a couple of kids. He had a number of affairs with women, he was seeing prostitutes, he was actively heterosexual, whether or not he was psychologically gay.

EB: I think that would be consistent with the times. He kept trying to be normal.

WS: But he actually had some intense relationships. He had fallen in love with Lillie Langtry, among others. And on his American tour, he fell in love with some woman in San Francisco. So the time frame of the book is a period long before his actively gay period, and I had no problem with the idea of him falling in love with a woman. There's a sex scene whose purpose, one of whose purposes, is to establish Oscar Wilde's heterosexual bona fides.

EB: At that point he may not have been all that ambiguous.

WS: People suspected him of being homosexual.

EB: But even now, that's automatic for anyone that's at all effeminate, who has effeminate gestures.

WS: Yeah, and he was constantly wearing outlandish costumes and saying outlandish things that "real men" wouldn't say. He became famous for a remark he made at Oxford before he ever actually did anything, produced anything. "I shall never be able to live up to my blue china," he said, and that remark was bandied about London. He was a celebrity simply for being who he was, so maybe in a sense he anticipated some of our twentieth-century celebrities.

EB: In other words, Andy Warhol would have loved him.

WS: He made his trip to the States partially because he'd been parodied in a Gilbert and Sullivan opera, and nobody in the States knew who Oscar Wilde was. D'oyly Carte, the producer of the play, arranged for Oscar to go on a lecture tour so that the American people had a chance to learn who Oscar was.

EB: So he helped lampoon himself. But the American lecture tour was something that was being done by English writers of the time. Dickens, a great critic of American art and society, made several American tours.

WS: Yes, but the neat thing was that Oscar was aware of the D'oyly Carte thing. He was showing the American people who *he* was so they could appreciate the character in the play, a parody of him. Which is an interesting notion. I would've liked to put that in the book, but there wasn't room. Every book I write, I try to throw in directly or indirectly everything I feel or know at a given time.

EB: Like throwing the Continental Op into *Miss Lizzie*.

WS: Right. As a kind of homage to Hammett. And most of the characters in *Lizzie* have names that originally belonged to private detectives. Annie Holmes, for example.

EB: Of course the newest thing is for writers to throw in the names of their friends, put them in as cab drivers, next-door neighbor, street names. I'm tickled to death that I'm a character in one of Hillerman's books. Jim Chee runs into me at a ceremony.

WS: I've done that. I put my friends John and Claudia Richards in *Wall of Glass*. And the woman I was living with, and Doug Higgins, an artist friend. It's fun.

It's nice to do your storytelling, that's the basic thing. And then it's nice to write the book as well as you possibly can, and it's nice to have another level where some other things are happening. It's nice, for example, to use the Continental Op. I get a kick out of it. It's nice to have a kind of hierarchy of meanings and possibilities.

On the simplest level, for example, a paragraph in a book should do a bunch of things all at once. It should advance the story, illuminate the characters, it should entertain the reader. And a book can do three or four things at once, on three or four different levels. I think that there's a lot going on in *Lizzie*—Amanda's coming of age, the slow unfolding of her personality. . . .

EB: Which is, I'm certain, why I like it so much. It's a great voice, the opening paragraph is wonderful.

WS: Thanks. For me, it's gratifying that the women who've read the book have liked it, that they've found Amanda a persuasive character.

EB: Obviously, you're not in danger of running out of historical characters.

WS: How did you like Daniel Begay as a Navajo, in *At Ease with the Dead*?

EB: I liked him a lot.

WS: You found him to be authentic?

EB: Yeah.

WS: I got a lot of help from the woman I was living with, who was a Navajo.

EB: I mentioned to you before, I was especially pleased with the scene at the lake. When you introduce this older Indian, right away I'm going, "Oh no, we're gonna get a

Photo by Ernie Bulow

little Castañeda, here. He's gonna be a mystic," and of course it's not there. When I got to the punch line "Did you wash your hand?" I about fell out of my chair. Wow, I've been tricked handsomely. You got me, cause I just knew you were gonna pull something stupid. I'm very touchy about people using Indian characters and doing it badly, partly because of Hillerman. My God, this stuff is coming out of the woodwork.

* * * *

EB: Has your publisher exercised much editorial control over the work you do?

WS: The only time St. Martin's has ever asked for any kind of major change was in *Wall of Glass,* at the end of the book, in the scene with Croft and the young girl. My editor felt that in the first version she came off a little too much like a Valley Girl. Generally I tend to believe that there's no such thing as constructive criticism, and my initial reaction was *"What?"* I work hard, anyone who does this work knows that it's difficult. If you care about it, you put everything you have into it. And sometimes you bleed over it. And so when someone tells me that, hey, this particular section doesn't work, I tend to bridle at first. But if what he says makes sense, then, after a day or two, usually, I'll see that it makes sense. And my editor was right, I finally realized, so I changed the scene.

* * * *

EB: You don't seem to be very political to me. I know a lot of mystery writers like to write political, a lot of them fancy that they right the world's wrongs. If child abuse is the topic of the day, you've got to write a child abuse book.

WS: I have a child abuse book coming up. *A Flower in the Desert.*

EB: So that one is more topical.

WS: Yeah. Everyone and her sister are writing books about child abuse. Well, it's a serious problem, and if it's being overemphasized right now, that's probably because it was underemphasized, or totally ignored, for so long. I think that my approach, if it could be described as anything, would probably be described as more religious than political. Politics don't particularly interest me. Politically, I'm probably your basic knee-jerk liberal, and I suppose that's reflected in my writing. But it's not something I think consciously about.

* * * *

EB: One of the things we haven't talked about that interests me: you must've given some thought as to why the mystery genre is so popular.

WS: I think in a time like ours, when values are being questioned and where certainties are hard to come by, mysteries can be very satisfying, because they presume, or they posit, some kind of stability. A mystery begins with some sort of tear in the social fabric. The warp and weave of society is somehow sundered. We could be talking about society at large, or some small microcosm of society—a neighborhood, a family. But something tears it apart. A murder, a theft, an embezzlement. Usually a murder. In any event, the fabric's been torn. It's up to the protagonist to figure out why and by whom it was torn. And, so far as he can, to reestablish order, to reweave the fabric. And I think that the notion that order *can* be restored, that the fabric *can* be rewoven, is a comforting one.

Personally, what I like about that metaphor, the fabric metaphor, is that whenever an actual fabric is repaired, rewoven, the fabric is never exactly what it was before it was torn. It's subtly different. And I think that if a mystery novel is a good one, the societal fabric, even though rewoven, is also subtly different. Things have changed slightly. Maybe even the protagonist, by virtue of what he's learned and done, has changed.

EB: We talked about the literary process but didn't get to the genre writers you most like.

WS: God, there's a whole bunch of them. There are so many good mystery writers out there. Chandler and Hammett, obviously. Nicholas Freeling. Josephine Tey. Reginald Hill. Janwillem van de Wetering.

EB: What about contemporary American writers?

WS: Lot of those I like, too. David Lindsay, for one.

EB: What do you like about Lindsay?

WS: He has a nice precision of detail. And psychologically, his characters are persuasive. His psychotics are always scary. And James Lee Burke, I think he's a fine writer.

EB: Again, someone struggling for many years to write what we think of as a more straight novel, literature. I mean he teaches, or did. An academic. I'm not sure he still does.

WS: Wasn't Parker an academic?

EB: There aren't a lot, by and large. It's interesting that a lot of the American academics tend to write in what might be called the hard-boiled style.

WS: Right. Whereas most of the English academics write cosies. Well, the hard-boiled style is originally, and maybe uniquely, American. But I like a lot of the Brits. Ruth Rendell, Peter Dickinson. Dickinson I admire because he tells a different story every single time. Each book has a different style, a different texture. I think he's got two or three books in a series—Inspector Pibble I think is the guy's name. But for the most part, each of them is a completely different book, in style, content, and approach from the one he did before.

EB: Not many writers can do that, it's true.

WS: It's not necessarily a wise thing to do, commercially.

EB: People like that comfort of a series character. As a matter of fact Dickinson's not collected.

WS: That's a pity. He's very good.

EB: Your historicals, with only two of them published so far, are establishing a sort of subgenre of their own, and even though the protagonists change from one novel to the next, they still have that series feel. As soon as someone reads a couple of them, he begins to have certain expectations.

WS: *Wilde West* hasn't been as successful as the most recent Croft book, and possibly that's something I have to think about.

EB: It may have simply been too daring.

WS: I really believed, when I wrote it, that the book would either get enormous acclaim, or that everyone would hate it. Either of which, naturally, would generate good sales. As you know, I got nice reviews, but the sales weren't so hot.

EB: I'm disappointed in that because I'm sure that we agree that its failure, or lack of enthusiasm on the part of book buyers, is a result of it not being solidly enough in the genre. But one of the things I have been excited about in recent years is that the genre seems to be very loose, broad, very flexible. But obviously there are some limits.

WS: For some readers, yeah. But on the other hand there are some readers who just got knocked out by it. So I don't know, you can't write to please everybody. . . .

EB: I have a feeling that it's a book that will eventually find a readership among people who don't normally read the genre.

WS: I hope so. But I think it's a book that will stand up over time. I liked it.

EB: I can certainly appreciate it more from a writer's point of view. Much tougher thing to do.

WS: I got a big kick out of doing this most recent Croft, and I'm really enjoying the one I'm doing now.

EB: The next one you talked to me about was the one with Houdini and Conan Doyle, which doesn't have a western theme. Are you interested in coming back to the West? Obviously it's pretty inexhaustible.

WS: If *Wilde West* had done better, I would've liked to spin briefly off somehow, maybe use some other historical character. There were so many neat people floating around then.

EB: Buffalo Bill.

WS: I thought about putting Buffalo Bill in *Wilde West*.

EB: If you read the Upwith biography of Custer, there were some political machinations and perhaps some land fraud he lent his name to.

WS: There are so many interesting characters in this country's history that you could use. In history in general. I once wanted to do a book about a guy who was investigating this early religion called Christianity. A Roman counsel or something. Have him meet Mary Magdalen.

The main reason I want to do Houdini and Conan Doyle is that the book would reveal another culture clash. Essentially it's a British manor house mystery in which Harry Houdini will be acting as a hard-boiled detective. And I like the idea, too, that I can play around with spiritualism again. Doyle was a firm believer, and Houdini wanted to be a believer.

The book'll be set in an interesting time, 1921, when England in particular was going through huge cultural changes. What's really interesting about that, for me, anyway, is here you have this really structured society that was beginning to show little ruptures and cracks. The book will be arranged like an English cozy, and it will be cerebral, I hope, but on the other hand you'll have this physical character who is, as I said, playing the part of the hard-boiled detective. It's playing with the genre as well, a reversal of *Wilde West,* in a way.

EB: Can you afford to take a chance on writing another one of your sport books? *Wilde West,* after all, hasn't done all that well.

WS: Yeah, well, you have to keep things moving. I'm not rich, by any means, not even particularly comfortable, financially, but I've got enough money coming in now that I can just do the writing. And if I'm writing, I might as well write what I want to write. Maybe, sooner or later, one of the books will break through and I'll become fabulously wealthy. But the only way it'll ever happen, if it does happen, is if I write what I'm comfortable writing. All the people who do produce breakthrough books aren't writing them with the idea of making a best-seller. They're writing what they want to, and they're writing it, usually, as well as they can.

EB: I'm not sure, for most people there never is a breakthrough. Hillerman just builds and builds and builds, gradually sells more and more copies.

WS: Someone told me—I don't know if this is true—that *Early Autumn* was supposed to be Robert Parker's breakthrough book. That's the one without Spencer. It's a novel about a guy and his wife and their friend who go up to a cottage in the woods somewhere. The book didn't do very well and Parker went back to Spencer.

Photo by Ernie Bulow

EB: His TV series came on at a time

that he was in decline. Certainly his last few books have not been well received. There are people who felt he'd written better, so the TV show had to be helping.

WS: His later books may not be as good as the early books, which I think are very fine. There's a lot of envy out there, and I've heard mystery writers complain that he's a terrible writer. Well, I think that even at his worst, he's pretty good. He writes some of the funniest dialogue around.

EB: I've heard fans complaining too, though. So what are your ambitions?

WS: I'd still like to do something that stretches me, like this Conan Doyle thing. And lately, it's occurred to me that I can stretch myself with the Croft books. I have to fill certain expectations with each book, that's part of the deal with the reader, but I can do other things, too, structurally.

EB: I'm sort of surprised that Santa Fe was lying in wait for you.

WS: There *have* been other mysteries set here. I think there was one in the fifties.

EB: Not very effective ones. They seemed to make very little use of cultures. There are a couple set in Albuquerque. There is at least one really great mystery by Richard Bradford's late wife, Lee Head, a writer that almost no one knows about. She wrote a really wonderful mystery set in Santa Fe called *The Crystal Clear Case.*

In terms of craftsmanship, you're happy writing murder mysteries?

WS: Yeah. So many terrific writers write murder mysteries, how can anyone feel it's a sellout to write mysteries? I've had people ask me, "Did you ever write a serious book?" I always want to ask them, "Did you ever ask a serious question?" I don't see where writing within a genre means you're not doing serious work. Homer was writing within a genre. So was Shakespeare. I think that it's only with the novel, in the eighteenth century, that the distinction began to be made. I really don't see why anyone at this point in time would make the distinction between serious literature and mystery or crime fiction.

* * * *

WS: As a reader of mysteries, I like it when somebody is doing something new and different, but I still want a crime there.

EB: I don't think that it's necessary that it be a murder.

WS: *The Daughter of Time.* Josephine Tey. Great book. It's about a pair of murders, but it's really more an investigation of the character of Richard III.

EB: Let's face it, a lot of the great serious novels involve crime.

WS: *Crime and Punishment. Hamlet.*

EB: Of course. Begins with a murder, he wasn't on the scene. That's the whole problem. Did they kill my old man.

WS: Because if they did, societally defined behavior requires that he . . .

EB: Societally defined, and, in my opinion there's some statecraft stuff there, too.

WS: The psychological thing, too. It's there, the ambivalent feeling he has for his father. And, as the Freudians like to point out, for his mother.

EB: Using the father, that was almost a Shakespearean motif, in the tragedies.

WS: My favorite Shakespeare is still *The Tempest.*

EB: Do you like Melville?

WS: Yeah. I've been thinking lately about re-reading *Moby Dick.*

EB: Remember to skip the whale chapters.

WS: Did you ever read *The Confidence Man?* I like the idea of John Ringman, the main character. He keeps changing identity throughout the book, and sometimes the clues that Melville gives you, to tell you that this new guy *is* Ringman, sometimes they're awfully subtle.

EB: Melville liked mysteries.

WS: Anyway, to get back to modern mysteries, I think the caliber of writing in the field is extraordinarily high right now. You've got people playing around with the genre and with people's expectations. Sometimes it doesn't work, but I think it's neat. There are some interesting, talented, skillful writers out there. It's nice to be a part of that.

EB: Especially with doing something new in the genre. I hope your publisher will alow you to continue to play with that.

WS: I'm not the first person to do that, there's the woman who used Samuel Johnson. Lillian de la Torre. She had him acting as a detective, with Boswell playing his Dr. Watson.

EB: Are you worried that we're coming into an age where literacy is so much on the decline you're not going to have an audience, no matter how well you write?

WS: A bit, yeah. Look at what it costs to buy a hardcover, or even a paperback book. Twenty bucks for a hardcover, six for a paperback. For six dollars, you can get three or four videos. Which, if you don't like reading, will occupy your time.

EB: And take no effort. Do you remember before television? For sort of accidental reasons, I didn't watch much TV before college.

WS: I remember by family getting its first TV. I used to watch a lot. I don't watch much now. Generally, I only watch the weather channel. This television is in effect a very expensive thermometer.

EB: There must be some things you watch.

WS: A few. I like "Mystery Science Fiction Theater 3000." And I like "Law and Order" and "Northern Exposure."

EB: What sorts of things do you use for inspiration?

WS: Writing. Seriously. As long as I'm working, ideas come all the time. I think it was Stan Getz who said that when you improvise, you open one door and you see that there are more doors behind that one. You keep opening doors. It's true of writing, too. So long as I'm writing, inspiration hasn't been a problem. Thank God.

EB: Hillerman said something of the same thing. He said usually by the time he's getting to the point of wrapping up a book either a character or idea has interested him. He almost always has a germ coming out of another, an idea that he simply can't explore.

WS: Exactly. There are writers, I've heard, who wait around for the light to descend around their shoulders, and then they do their work. I don't know how they pull it off. Or, in fact, *if* they do.

*   *   *   *

EB: Okay. Let's talk about clichés. In all the Santa Fe books, Croft is a smartass. You make the observation that most of his comments are internal. He says smart things but he doesn't say them to the character, except sometimes to Rita.

WS: For the most part he doesn't put down people to their faces. He thinks his wiseass remark and the reader knows about it.

EB: It does make a difference; it makes him a little more humane. But he swims laps, he plays racquetball, he has a cop friend, Hector, who almost becomes a cliché. You mentioned the hooded eyes, the Frito Bandito mustache. Then at the end of the first chapter the first guy is already dead, which is good; I always thought that the ultimate would be to have the murder in the opening line.

WS: I've always wanted to put the clue that solves the crime into the opening paragraph, and not have anyone aware of it until the end.

EB: John Dixon Carr could have done it.

WS: Probably, yeah. He was good. I did get a little irritated, whenever I read him, by the fact that nobody ever *said* anything. They *cried* it, they *retorted* it. . . .

EB: The Tom Swift school of writing. But back to Joshua. Joshua doesn't carry a gun.

WS: He's not allowed to carry a gun. In New Mexico, private investigators can't get a carry permit. No one can. If Croft carries a gun and it's not visible, it's illegal.

EB: That's odd, because you think of the West . . . when I was a kid in Ely, Nevada, you could wear a gun.

WS: You can wear a gun in New Mexico.

EB: You have to wear it western style, in a holster.

WS: You can wear it scotchtaped to your forehead. In fact, Grober, my first New Mexico PI, says something like that in a short story. As long as it's visible. But there are no concealed weapon permits in New Mexico. Croft doesn't like guns anyway. Wearing a gun, he says, would spoil the drape of his jacket.

EB: Almost every one of those first chapters ends literally with a bang, the window being shot out, or him being slugged.

WS: I like that convention, having a hook at the end of each chapter. I tend to do that consciously.

EB: Well, it's in the tradition. Also the bit in the opening chapters on the police procedural stuff, which then disappears.

WS: It's not necessary. When I wrote it, I made sure that what I said about the Santa Fe Police Department was accurate. But once it gets mentioned, it doesn't get mentioned again. I'm really not all that interested in police procedure, or I wasn't for that book. And for that book, knowing a lot about it wasn't necessary.

EB: Reading this, I was struck by two things. It was very formulaic, and there was a definite break point about halfway. The book turns around, or changes. Now in all fairness, that doesn't mean that it's not a fun read to the midpoint, it's just that it's not Walter Satterthwait, except for the clever repartee. Then it takes off.

Photo by Ernie Bulow

WS: The book began, really, to fill the contractual obligation I had with St. Martin's. The first book I sold to them, in outline, just fell apart when I was in Greece, and I owed them a book. So I started *Wall of Glass,* and about halfway through, I started really liking the characters in it. If the book pays off, that may have something to do with the plot having been set up before I wrote the thing.

EB: In the second book there's more development, and I gather that Croft continues to develop. I wonder, did it occur to you to go back and make any changes to him?

WS: That first book was written under enormous difficulty. My personal relationship was falling apart, I was working four or five nights a week as a bartender, so I really can't remember the actual process of writing it. I remember finishing it, and I remember that there was a point, in writing it, where I said to myself, I really like these people. Maybe that did change my attitude.

EB: Other things change, as well. There's more use of the landscape, for example. The Hispanics are less clichéd and more interesting.

WS: Writing is always on-the-job training. Maybe halfway through that book I started to see what I was doing.

EB: The bar scene in Truchas, for example, was much better writing than the first half. Obviously you were getting a feel. What about your Hispanic Zen master?

WS: He's one of the driving forces of the book, isn't he? He shows up again in the third Croft book, *A Flower in the Desert.* It's neat to invent a character you like, and then be able to bring him back. I'd like to bring back Daniel Begay, from *At Ease with the Dead.*

EB: He's wonderful. He definitely is not a cliché. Not what you'd expect at all.

Another thing about *Wall of Glass* is it almost seems like overkill. Until the reader gets to the end he doesn't know he's been had. I think that book ends nicely. It's almost a case of overload there, because you had the robbery and these two strongarm guys, who are real badasses, then you have the porno stuff, and as it turns out it doesn't have that much to do with it, but it's a good red herring, then the grave robbing, so you have a minimum of four crimes and that's if you don't count murders.

WS: The grave robbing is the major thing. I knew I was going to do the Indian stuff in the beginning. The grave robbing was in the outline. But in the process of researching that, I began to feel it was important to get across to people that this is a serious problem, morally and economically, for the Indians.

EB: You kind of flog the Germans, too. Some rather nasty characters. The French consume American Indian stuff almost as much as they do.

WS: Yeah, I confess to a kind of prejudice. I remember once, when I was in Greece, I was talking to a very attractive woman who happened to be German, and she mentioned that her father had worked with Von Braun on the V-2 rocket. I asked her, how does it feel to be the daughter of that generation? She said, "Well, it's very difficult, of course, terrible, but you have to understand that a lot of that stuff has been exaggerated by the Jewish producers in Hollywood." I said, "Right. Excuse me, I have to go peel an orange."

EB: This is not meant to be bashing the book, but the Leightons, the couple in *Wall of Glass,* they also seem to be a bit cliché ridden. He's a promoter, a builder, which in this town is nearly tantamount to being a Nazi or a dim-witted bully, and she's a bored dipso who's into kinky sex, and with the two of them you have a very unlovely but recognizable couple. They also contribute to that clichéd atmosphere.

WS: Well, both the Leightons do show another side of their characters later on in the book. I think the ending does work. The only book about which anyone said he thought he knew who did it before the end was *Wilde West.*

EB: As I've said, I hardly read mysteries for the mystery anymore. I just like them because they have plots, which so much contemporary literature doesn't, and often very interesting characterizations. That's developing in the later books.

WS: I like to think I'm becoming a better writer too. I'm still out there looking at people. Even Germans. I do tend to bash Germans in my work. That's something I have to watch. If I use a German character who's also an academic, then the reader will know in a shot that he's the guilty party.

EB: I keep hoping you won't trot out a single academic. Not a single one. Let's talk about *Wilde West*. My only disappointment with *Wilde West* is that the marshal turns out to be pretty lame. You keep hoping for more from him, but since Wilde has to be the one to resolve the mystery, what could you do?

WS: I don't really think he's all that lame. He's an alcoholic and, primarily as a result of his alcoholism, he screws up. On the rare occasions when he's sober, he does okay. And, within the context of the time, he's a fairly liberal guy. I liked him as a character.

EB: You mix violence with sex in *Wilde West*.

WS: One of the main characters is a serial killer. Mixing sex with violence, from what we know about serial killers, is something that many of them do.

EB: The sex elements in the murder scenes are so surgical that they don't strike the reader as being particularly sexual.

WS: Sure. But in real life, with real serial killers, there's almost invariably a sexual element.

EB: Well, you know, the theory now is that violent sex crimes, they're not sex crimes at all.

WS: I'm no psychologist, obviously, but I think that's overstating it. If the only element were violence, the guy could just punch the shit out of his victim. Usually, he does something else, something sexual. To say that rape, for example, has nothing to do with sex is to romanticize sex, I think, to redefine it as one specific romantic thing. For me, it seems obvious that there's a sexual element in rape. It may be violence, but it's his penis he's using, not his fist. I'm not saying that that's a good thing, it's not, it's a terrible thing, maybe worse than using his fist. But that fact is, he didn't sit down and figure out: "Let's see, I wanna be violent. I wanna hurt this woman. Do I use my fist or do I use my penis?" He's got, clearly, a lot of problems, a lot of compulsions, and some of them are sexual. People aren't really compartmentalized. The compartmentalization we all use, to talk about ourselves and other people, is just a kind of handy fiction. That was love, that was sex, that was economics. They're just handles we attach to things so we can manipulate them, move them around mentally. Any problem in one area of someone's life will spill over into the other areas.

EB: Tell me about the serial killer. You're doing dual things there, because the serial killer, besides the extraordinary exceptions such as Jack the Ripper, is a fairly recent phenomenon, as far as we know.

WS: There was a guy named Blodgins who was killing women at the Chicago World's Fair, in the 1890s. He built his house with chutes and secret passageways that led into a gas chamber and a vat of acid. I'm not sure that serial killing, killing more than one person in a ritualized way, is all that recent a phenomenon. There've probably been more of them per capita, and there are more people.

EB: But things like the freeway shooting, for example. That's got to be a very contemporary phenomenon. We've just never had that kind of stress in the past. You mentioned having to go back, after you wrote the opening of the book, and make the killings more horrific. Was that a stressful thing for you?

WS: Yeah. It was stressful to know that I could find that kind of blackness inside my head. I think all of us have monsters dwelling in the back of our mind. People like Stephen King tackle them on a regular basis. I don't have to, usually, but I did in this case. For a couple of weeks after I wrote those things, I didn't sleep very well. I wanted the serial killer scenes to be really rough, even knowing at the time I wrote it that it would perhaps damage sales of a book that was, in my opinion, essentially a comedy. Because that book *is* a comedy. Even by Aristotelian definitions, it's a comedy. An outrageous comedy, maybe, with something to offend just about everyone, but a comedy.

EB: It's definitely outrageous. I enjoyed almost everything about it, though. I didn't particularly mind the mix. You give the serial killer some of the most compassionate dialogue in the book. The most spiritual. Why?

WS: Well, I think it's possible to be an absolute monster and still say things that happen to be true. And remember, he's not consciously a bad person. His conscious self, the only one he's aware of, is basically religious.

EB: In *Miss Lizzie* and *Wilde West,* you raise the question of evil, and then you're so ambivalent about it. In both cases, you're saying that the character could be a nice, admirable person and still have this dark side.

WS: Yeah.

EB: Does this, then, put you in a realm where "the Devil does it"? I guess the question is what is the nature of evil for you?

WS: That's a question that's addressed—if not answered, maybe—in the new Croft book, by Montoya, my Zen Hispanic Godfather. He tells Croft that he believes that all people and all things are essentially Buddha, by nature good, wonderful, fine, perfect, but that there are patterns in human activity into which you can fall because of the three follies: ignorance, greed, or anger. I'll buy that. Greed, in particular, is a powerful impetus. A lot of the stuff that happens in my books, greed is the motivator.

EB: How can pure evil and goodness be in the same person?

WS: I think it's inevitable that they be. I don't think that there's anybody in the world who's untainted by evil or untouched by grace. I suppose it's possible that there are perfectly good people in the world . . . Mother Theresa, for example. But for all I know, this woman is plotting something.

EB: Montoya talks about Killebrew in the first book. Croft says to him, maybe he'll come back as a mollusk or something, and Montoya says that would be an improvement. It's something that you've addressed in every book.

WS: It's part of my beliefs that people are mixtures of good and evil, that there's probably no such thing as pure evil. Or, as I say, pure good. What's interesting to me is the mixture, and the dynamics of the mixture.

EB: You've mentioned Buddhism several times. Would you describe yourself as a practicing Buddhist?

WS: Yeah. And I'm going to keep practicing until I get it right.

EB: You want to talk about it?

WS: Buddhism isn't something, finally, that you can talk about, except by indirection.

EB: So what is it? Indirectly.

WS: Beats me.

EB: What would you like to see written on your gravestone?

WS: Someone else's name.

EB: Seriously.

WS: Seriously? I don't know. *He paid his bar tab?* Or how about *Wit's End?*

The African Stories

As he tells us in his interview, Walter Satterthwait first went to Africa simply because it was an isolated and inexpensive place to live while he finished a book. Warned by this first agent not to try to sell a novel about Africa because nobody wanted to read about it, Satterthwait was able to sell short stories set in Africa, one of which is reprinted here from *Alfred Hitchcock's Mystery Magazine.*

Satterthwait says, "I simply set out to write the best story I could, which was the first of the African stories, 'A Conflict of Interest.' I named my detective for the African houseboy in Lamu, Andrew. Over the next five or six years I wrote one a year for *Hitchcock Magazine."* Satterthwait was finally writing short stories that sold and says today that he would like to find time to do more of them. He describes his relationship with his editor at *Hitchcock* as very pleasant.

Though none of the stories actually mentions Kenya, Mombasa is sometimes referred to as the nearest large city to the township where the stories take place, somewhere on the African coast. His character, Andrew Mbutu, a sergeant with the local constabulary, is a member of the Giriami tribe, a minority in the country, which puts Andrew in a defensive position. Kenya is largely run by Kikuyus who look down on the Giriami. Andrew is mission-educated, and a major premise of the stories is that he is brighter than most of the people he has to work with.

Andrew Mbutu, in spite of his minority status, has no chip on his shoulder. He loves being a constable, understands thoroughly the bureaucracy he is forced to deal with, and calmly and efficiently solves his cases. We never learn a great deal about him in the stories; he is thirtyish, married with children, afraid of heights, and gets around town on a moped when he isn't driven in an official vehicle by his assistant, Constable Kobari, a Kikuyu. Kobari drives a car like a racetrack maniac and seldom gives Mbutu much help in solving crimes. They are supported by a nice set of recurrent characters including the wonderfully stupid and affected Cadet Inspector Moi, who is nominally his superior but who is inferior to him in every way and a constant thorn in his side. Moi runs around in pastel jump suits and a goatee which is "vaguely obscene." Moi is not only Kikuyu, but once spent a year in England with Scotland Yard, which gave him a ridiculously inflated opinion of himself. He always opts for the simple, obvious, and incorrect solution to the cases.

The most wonderful of the recurring supporting cast is the Indian Doctor Murmajee, who acts as the pathologist and medical examiner. Doctor Murmajee, considered Asian by the Africans, speaks in a singsong voice that Andrew considers very annoying, and he drives Mbutu crazy with his conservative reluctance to formulate an opinion quickly on any fact, even the most obvious. He even hesitates to pronounce victims of violent death as dead at the scene, refusing to pass judgment on anything before he performs his autopsies. And his greatest love in life, apparently, is to perform autopsies on Europeans, betraying a fascination with their innards "as though he expected to find, hidden away among them, some hitherto overlooked gland whose secretions produced white skins, internal combustion engines, computers, imperialism."

There is a nice feel of authenticity to the African stories. Swahili is the lingua franca of the country, and Satterthwait scatters native words through the tales, adding verisimilitude and interest. Besides the dominant Kikuyus and the humbler Giriamis, other tribes featured in the stories are the Somalis, who supply large numbers of beautiful women to the prostitute class, and the famed Masai, who are both warriors and witch doctors. "A Conflict of Interest" and "To Catch a Wizard" make use of native medicine and magic. The moccasin telegraph idea is important in "The Gold of Miyani." Satterthwait insists that there isn't a great deal of ethnological material in the stories, nor much research, but simply things he picked up by living in Africa for a time.

Andrew's racial status becomes clearer in the story "The Smoke People," in which a group of Giriamis, an extended family, are caretakers of the city dump and live amid the burning rubbish. This is based on actual observation, but in real life there are more people in the family and they keep livestock with them in their smoky land of refuse. "The Smoke People" is another of Walter's stories in which the person responsible for the "murder" is never punished, a development based on Andrew's personal judgment. The theme of legal guilt versus moral responsibility is recurrent in Satterthwait's writing. The worst of the villains in "To Catch a Wizard" is also beyond the reach of legal punishment, which Walter rightly insists is often the case in real life, but less satisfying in the mystery genre where wrongs are often righted outside the slow and unpredictable workings of the legal system.

In the African stories the crimes are always against and usually by Europeans—*wazungu*—a designation that includes Americans. The colonialist whites are often crude and cruel to nonwhites; they are insensitive to the environment (for example, they poach ivory); they are alcoholics and womanizers. The plots of several of the stories hinge on overactive libidos: Atlee in "The Gold of Miyani" has "slept with half the women in the country, African and European alike" while the victim in "To Catch a Wizard" is living with a Somali prostitute and the victim in "A Conflict of Interest" has been forcing himself on his son's wife.

It was extremely difficult to choose which story to include here, partly because there are no weak tales in the series. I settled on "Make No Mistake" (1989) for a couple of reasons. Most of the series characters are present here with the bonus appearance of a Satterthwait regular, a detective patterned on Dashiell Hammett's Continental Op. The heavy-drinking Bwana Emerson is a persona who recurs often in Walter's work. Emerson is first noted by the chief with the observation "He looks rather like a clown, but I very much suspect he's not." The self-deprecating appearance is the signature of the anonymous operative from Hammett's short stories. Being short, fat, and untidy can be useful on a case when it causes the opposition to badly underestimate his intelligence and abilities.

"Emerson's shoes were scuffed, his shirt and tie spotted with soup stains, and his suit looked as though it had been used to haul rocks," writes Satterthwait, and elsewhere he adds, "His broad face was red, the cheeks and nose alight with a fine network of capillaries." Though Andrew has virtually solved the crime when Emerson appears on the scene, the American (probably a CIA agent) can lean on other Americans and find out things through diplomatic channels which are denied the black detective. As usual when his character appears, an astute, wise-talking tough guy hides behind the rumpled, dowdy exterior.

Another signature touch to the Satterthwait short story is a penchant for O. Henry–esque endings featuring double and triple twists, a holdover from his years of penning classically constructed short stories. These surprise endings, however, rely more on a strong sense of irony and a twisted sense of reality than on the kind of pure trick that O. Henry himself was so fond of, though a trick is definitely part of "Make No Mistake."

Just for fun Walter throws in references to other detectives: Bulldog Drummond in "Make No Mistakes," Sherlock Holmes in "A Conflict of Interest," and Mike Hammer in "Gold of Miyani." For readers who enjoy that sort of thing, check out characters' names in *Miss Lizzie* and elsewhere. As Walter says, beyond telling a good story and entertaining the readers, and maybe even providing a provocative bit of philosophy, the writer ought to be able to have fun—add another dimension to the work.

The last short story so far in the series, "The Gold of Miyani," is taken from the abandoned novel and features a fascinating overlay of African history from the years of political liberation. Walter rightly considers his African stories to be some of his best writing, and it is likely that a publisher will collect the tales and issue them together in a single volume. Satterthwait would like to add to the series if he could afford to take time from his novel writing. Collectively the African stories deserve a reputation, not just as fine short stories, but for the creation of an ethnic detective who could rank with Arthur Upfield's aboriginal Napoleon Bonaparte or Hillerman's Jim Chee.

MakeNo**Mistake**

Working with their customary speed and flair, the Technical Unit had needed only twenty minutes to reduce the suite of rooms to a shambles. Here in the sitting room, tables were overturned, chairs were sprawling. Fingerprint powder lay in small arctic drifts in the corners; cloudy flashbulbs littered the floor like the issue of an extremely befuddled hen.

And there, lying on the rug at the base of the open french door, was the sniper rifle. Even dusted over with a fine coating of powder, like a cruller, it still looked lean and lethal.

As indeed it should. Just over an hour before, it had sent a high-powered slug shrieking through the air into the suddenly fragile skull of a Mr. Forrest Tupperman, a tourist from Tarpon Springs, Florida, wherever and whatever that might be.

"No prints at all?" Sergeant Andrew Mbutu asked young Constable Umwayo, who squatted beside the weapon, about to slip it into a plastic garbage bag.

"None, sergeant," said Umwayo, looking up and pouting. (He was inconsolable whenever the marvels of technology failed him.) "None on the gun itself, none on the scope, and none anywhere else in the room."

"She wiped them all off before she left."

"Yes," nodded Umwayo sadly. "Yes, so it would seem."

Andrew frowned. "What sort of woman uses a rifle like that?"

"Not mine," said Umwayo, and then suddenly cupping his hand over his mouth to hide his bad teeth, he tittered and added, "I hope."

Andrew nodded, distracted, and stepped through the open french doors onto the balcony. His stomach rising in a giddy rush to the back of his head—he *hated* heights—he peered over the railing at the people who scurried up and down Harambee Street, far below.

Tourists. Even the drought of the past few years, and the famine that followed it, had not stopped them. (Although, to be sure, the AIDS epidemic had rather slowed down the Sex Trips from Scandinavia.) Each year now they came in ever-increasing numbers, from Europe, from America, from Japan, flooding into the Township by car and boat, by train and plane. All of them had helped to change the place, slowly but inexorably, from a quiet fishing port to a kind of Third World amusement park inhabited by Genuine African Natives. And now, as though not adequately entertained by sand and sun and gimcrack souvenirs, they were carting along high-powered rifles to dispatch each other.

An idea, perhaps, whose time had come. Perhaps the Tourism Ministry should have someone at the arrivals gate at the airport, cheerfully issuing guns and ammunition to the passengers as they deplaned. "Good hunting, bwana. Have a nice day."

Why stop at guns? Why not hand grenades? Bazookas? Tactical nuclear weapons?

Andrew turned and looked up the wall of the hotel, varnished a pale gold now by the light of the setting sun. Twenty-four dizzy stories from bottom to top.

A Saudi prince had erected this tower of elegance, all marble and glass and chilly air-conditioned splendor overlooking the Indian Ocean: the Soroya (named after his wife). He had erected, too, the building's twin, a duplicate hotel: the Jasmine (after his mistress). Both totally self-contained, each held its own shops, boutiques, discos, and restaurants where such genuine African cuisine as buffalo *flambé* was served by former Nairobi gigolos wearing tuxedos and smarmy smiles.

The two buildings were separated one from another by three blocks of Harambee Street, a distance of a hundred meters. Precisely the distance, as today's events had established, of a well-placed shot from a sniper rifle.

Staring off at the Jasmine, Andrew saw a squat individual suddenly emerge onto a balcony set at approximately the same height above street level as his own. Wearing civilian clothes, he was a small dark figure against the facade of the building.

Too far away to tell, of course, but probably Hasdruble Inye of the CID, investigating the murder scene. Which meant that Inye's immediate superior, the inestimable Cadet Inspector Moi, would not be far behind. Yes, there: a sudden flash of cerulean blue as Moi (as what could *only* be Moi, resplendent in yet another of his legendary pastel jumpsuits) stepped out onto the balcony.

Well. Better get this done before the cadet inspector shows up here. That body at the Jasmine won't hold him forever.

He turned and walked back into the hotel room. Crossed the carpet and stalked into the bedroom.

The dresser overturned, the bed torn apart as though slept in by a claustrophobe. More puffy camera eggs scattered about.

Standing by the closet, Constables Ngio and Gona giggled as each held up, against himself, one of the woman's dresses and preened before the mirror. Eyelashes were elaborately batting, lips seductively puckering. Constable Gona, built like a water buffalo, looked particularly appealing.

Completely hopeless. Keystone Kops, both of them.

Andrew turned and stalked back into the sitting room.

None of this made any sense. Everything here, the rifle, the distance and accuracy of the shot, the removal of latent prints, suggested a professional. Perhaps a political kill? Kennedy in Dallas. Martin Luther King in . . . where was it? Somewhere in the American south.

What had this Forrest Tupperman done to deserve such an ending? (What sort of a name was Tupperman, anyway? What sort of a name was *Forrest?*)

And a woman assassin?

CIA? The CIA no doubt had teams of women assassins. An equal opportunity employer, was it not? Probably recruited them at the Olympics, offered them free steroids for the rest of their lives. Did marksmen— markswomen? markspersons?—take steroids?

Had Tupperman run afoul of the CIA?

Andrew glanced at his watch. Where *was* Kobari? Send him on one simple errand and, abracadabra, he disappears.

As though somehow preternaturally aware of this slander, Constable Kobari at that moment opened the front door and entered the suite. He grinned at Andrew and announced, "Sergeant, we have another witness." He turned and beckoned toward someone standing out in the hall.

She stepped in warily, eyes darting, a small, slight, elderly woman in the black and orange uniform of a maid. When her glance found Andrew, she frowned and took an involuntary step backward.

"Ah," said Andrew, and smiled happily at the woman. "Ruth. How is business?"

She scowled. "I have a job now."

Constable Kobari, puzzled, looked back and forth between them. He said, "You know her, sergeant?"

"Certainly," Andrew smiled. "Ruth Awante. A most accomplished pickpocket." To the woman: "But I understand that you were in Nairobi, Ruth. What happened? Did you find that the climate didn't agree with you?"

No longer cowed, holding high her grizzled head, she answered in Swahili, "I have changed my ways."

"Yes?" said Andrew in the same language. "An upstanding citizen these days, is it?"

A small stiff nod. *"Ndio."* Yes.

"Then I'm sure you'll be glad to help us. Come. Sit down."

Through some oversight on the part of the Technical Unit, the furniture in the dining area was still upright. Andrew and Kobari sat side by side; the woman, sulking, eyes lowered, sat opposite them, across the round table.

"Now," said Andrew, slipping his notebook and pen from his shirt pocket. "You say you're a witness."

She shifted in her seat, and jerked her thumb toward Constable Kobari. *"He* says I'm a witness."

"I spoke with the one they call the head steward," Kobari told Andrew. "As you advised. He said she was assigned to clean the hallway, outside, between four thirty and five thirty."

Andrew nodded. The shot, according to the other witnesses, had come at five o'clock. He asked Ruth Awante, "So you were outside, in the hallway, when the shot was fired?"

She shrugged, her face sullen. "Perhaps I was, perhaps I wasn't."

Andrew nodded. "And perhaps I shall inform the head steward of your very interesting past."

Frowning again, she dug her right hand into her maid's apron, pulled out a crumped pack of cigarettes and a disposable plastic lighter. "I can smoke?"

Andrew shrugged.

She stuck a cigarette between her lips, lighted it. With gnarled finger and thumb she plucked the cigarette away and narrowed her eyes against the smoke. She saw Andrew avert his glance from her hand, and deliberately, almost scornfully, she held it out so he could see the knobby joints. "I can no longer live the old way. I have the arthritis."

Andrew nodded; he had realized as soon as he saw the fingers curved like talons. He pushed a square glass ashtray across the table, toward her.

She notched the cigarette into the groove in the ashtray and put her hands in her lap below the table, as though hiding them. She looked at him levelly. "If I tell you," she said, "shall I be paid?"

"No," said Andrew. "Of course not. But if you tell the truth, I shall be happy to forget your former occupation."

She scowled. "You are worse than the Asians." She meant the Indian merchants who owned the local *dukas,* the shops, and who were considered, by most of the Township's Africans, to be licensed bandits.

"You were out there," Andrew said. "In the hallway."

After a moment, she nodded. *"Ndio."* She lifted her hand above the table, picked up the cigarette, puffed on it.

"You heard the shot," Andrew said, and flipped open the notebook.

She exhaled a pale blue plume of smoke. "At about the eleventh hour." Five o'clock. "I did not know it was a shot. I thought that someone had dropped something. In one of the rooms."

"Did you see anything?"

"I saw her. Earlier."

"Her. You mean Jeannette Moseley? The woman who was staying in this room?"

A nod.

"When?"

"Just as I came to the hallway. She was coming in here."

"So at the tenth hour and one half." Four thirty.

A nod.

"How did you know it was she?"

"I had seen her before. Yesterday and the day before."

"Describe her."

Ruth Awante did. A tall, slender, brunette woman with brown eyes. One of the *Wazungu,* a word which meant Europeans, or by extension Americans.

Andrew nodded; this matched the description he had been given by the hotel desk clerk, and which he had already phoned in to the station.

He asked her, "What did you see after you heard the shot?"

"Nothing."

"How long did you remain in the hallway?"

"Until I saw the *polisi* come." Constable Gona, the first police officer on the scene. But Gona had found the room empty. . . .

"You did not see her leave the room? The Moseley woman?"

Ruth Awante shook her head.

"You were in the hallway the entire time?"

A nod.

"Could she have left this floor by some other way?"

Another shake of her head. "To reach the elevator or the stairs, she would have had to pass by me."

It was just barely possible, given some elaborate gymnastics, that the woman might have swung from the balcony of her suite to one of the balconies adjoining it. But the room to the east was occupied by the French couple, Mr. and Mrs. Danon, who had first reported the sound of the shot. Andrew had spoken with them; they had received no unexpected guests via their balcony.

The suite to the west was unoccupied, the door to the balcony locked from within. Theoretically, of course, the woman could have earlier broken into the empty rooms and unlocked the balcony door; and then, after bringing down the hapless Mr. Tupperman from her own suite, leaped over to the empty one. Locked all the doors behind her when she left.

But to what end? Simply to provide a conundrum?

And she would, anyway, still have had to pass by Ruth Awante.

Ropes? Rapelling down the hotel's side like a mountain climber? Any woman who could use a high-powered rifle might be capable of such a stunt.

But no ropes in her room, no evidence of any; and someone, without a doubt, would have witnessed the performance. No one had.

Whatever she had done after she fired the rifle, she was no longer on the twelfth floor. Every room, every maintenance closet, had been checked by the constabulary, under Andrew's supervision.

"Did you see anyone else in the hallway?"

She moved her bony shoulders in an indifferent shrug. "Two men."

"Guests of the hotel?"

"One was. I have seen him here before. Downstairs, on the first floor."

"In which room was he staying?"

Another shrug. "I do not know. I saw him only when he went by to get the elevator."

"And the other man?"

"Him I have not seen before."

"Describe these men."

She said that both were *Wazungu*. The man whom she had seen before was short, heavyset, of average height, in his thirties, wearing shorts and a brightly colored shirt. Brown hair, brown eyes. The second man was taller, thinner, approximately the same age, wearing a khaki safari suit. Short blond hair, blue eyes, glasses.

Andrew asked her, "At what time did you see these two?"

"Before the *polisi* came."

"After the shot was fired?"

"*Ndio.*"

Andrew turned to Constable Kobari. "Go with her down to the front desk. See if the clerk can identify these men."

Kobari nodded. "You think they may have been involved, sergeant?"

"I do not know. But even if not, they may have seen something."

After Kobari and the woman left, Andrew strolled through the apartment once more. The sitting room, the bedroom, finally the bathroom.

More fingerprint powder in here. But, just as in the rest of the suite, no fingerprints.

Andrew opened the door to the medicine cabinet and peered in. It told him no more now than it had when he first examined it. Only that she had left without her perfumes, her creams, her powders.

He looked at the bathtub. The Technical Unit had found in it not a single strand of Jeannette Moseley's hair. Except for the cosmetics, and for the clothes and the suitcase in the closet, it was as though Jeannette Moseley had never existed.

Andrew glanced at the toilet, at the uplifted seat, and suddenly he frowned.

He stalked back out to the sitting room, where Constable Umwayo, bending over the sofa, was snapping his briefcase shut.

"Umwayo," he said.

"Sergeant?"

"You dusted for prints on the toilet seat?"

"Yes, of course." Umwayo straightened up and slapped powder from the front of his uniform slacks.

"Was the seat up or down when you did?"

Once again cupping his hand over his mouth, Umwayo giggled.

A policeman, a member of the Technical Unit; and toilets made him giggle. "It's a simple question, man. When you first saw the seat, was it up or down?"

"Oh," Umwayo said quickly, suddenly serious. "Up. It was up, sergeant. Why?"

"You were the first one in there?"

"Yes."

"What about Constable Gona?"

"I arrived only a few minutes after Gona. I don't think—"

Andrew turned and stalked into the bedroom. Gona and Ngio had stopped playing simpering damsels and had finished packing the woman's clothing in the suitcase. To Gona, Andrew said, "Did you touch the toilet since you've been here?"

Gona blinked at him. "What?"

Imbecile. "Did you touch the bloody toilet?"

Gona scowled, resentful. Although officially his superior, Andrew was a Giriama tribesman and by definition inferior to a dauntless Kikuyu warrior like himself. "Why would I touch the toilet? Am I a janitor?"

Andrew frowned: not yet, not yet. He turned to Ngio. "Did you?"

Ngio, fellow Giriama, seemed merely baffled. He looked from Andrew to Gona, back again to Andrew. "No, sergeant. Was I supposed to?"

Andrew strode across the room toward the telephone on the nightstand. Just as his hand reached it, it rang.

He snatched it up. *"Jambo,"* he snapped into the receiver.

"Put Mbutu on, would you." The plummy languid tones of Inspector Moi, who had spent an exchange year with Scotland Yard and who fancied himself Bulldog Drummond.

"This is Sergeant Mbutu, inspector."

"Ah. Good man. About finished up over there, are you? We've wrapped it up at this end. Thought it was time we compared notes, eh?"

"Inspector, I believe I know how we can locate this Jeannette Moseley."

"Indeed? Left a forwarding address, did she? Ha ha."

The two constables were staring at Andrew like a pair of cinema buffoons, their mouths agape. Wincing with impatience, he waved them away. They looked at each other in identical confusion, shrugged in identical resignation. Then, comics to the end, they grabbed simultaneously at the suitcase. After only an instant, Gona twisted it away, Ngio gave Andrew a wounded look, and the two of them shuffled off.

"Still there, sergeant?"

"Inspector, we must stop looking for a woman."

"Come again?"

"There is no Jeannette Moseley. There never was."

A silence at the other end. Then Moi cleared his throat. "Didn't quite catch that, sergeant."

"There is no Jeannette Moseley. The toilet, inspector. The seat was up."

"The seat was up," Moi repeated blankly. Andrew could picture him, his eyes empty, his mouth parted in stupefaction above the neatly trimmed goatee.

"Yes," said Andrew. "No one else has touched it. And there'd be no reason for a woman to lift up the toilet seat. A man might, but a woman, never."

"Sergeant, I *am* acquainted with the, ah, anatomical differences between men and women. Been married, after all, for five years now."

Which, given Moi's observational skills, established absolutely nothing. "Yes, of course, inspector, but—"

"People have *seen* this woman," said Moi. "I've spoken by telephone to the desk clerk, and he checked her into the hotel himself. Spoke with Constable Gona before you got there—good man, Gona—and he tells me her stuff was still all over the suite. Dresses, skirts, that sort of thing. So she's hardly a figment of the imagination, eh? Ha ha." Andrew rolled his eyes. Moi and Gona. Giants still walked the earth.

He said, "What the desk clerk saw, inspector, was a man dressed as a woman. There was a maid in the hallway at the time of the shooting. No one passed by her except two men. One of them had to be this Jeannette Moseley."

"Come now," interrupted Moi. "You've got all that on the word of some hotel maid?"

"I know the maid, inspector. She has an excellent eye." As would any good pickpocket, a fact which, under the circumstances, Andrew forbore to mention.

"Now look here, sergeant," said Moi. "I'm perfectly satisfied that I've uncovered the motive in this business, and, make no mistake, it has nothing to do with your transvestite."

Andrew sighed. Discreetly, swiveling the mouthpiece briefly away. "Yes?"

"What we have here is a case of jealousy. Pure and simple."

"Jealousy," Andrew repeated, and realized that his own mouth had parted in stupefaction. He closed it.

"This Tupperman chap," said Moi, "was having at it with some mopsy in the States. Got that straight from the horses' mouth. The wife. Horse is putting it mildly. Ha ha. Hyena, more like it. No accounting for taste, eh? Anyway, she found out about the slap and tickle, nearly divorced him. Then the two of them decided to give it another go, and came out here to get away from the mess. Obviously, the mopsy followed and waited till she had her chance, and then, *bang*, no more Bwana Tupperman."

After another discreet sigh, Andrew asked, "Does the wife have a name for this person?"

"Gladys Norman. Tupperman's secretary. Description matches Moseley's. All we have to do is find her and we're home free."

"But, inspector—"

"Meantime, the American Embassy is sending someone down on the seven-thirty plane. Attaché of some sort. Name of Emerson. Get a move on and you'll just have time to meet him at the airport. Bring him round to the station and I'll fill him in. And, Mbutu, let's not have any talk in the car about transvestites. Or *toilets*, for God's sake." Moi's shudder was audible. "Not in front of embassy people."

The desk clerk had identified the first of the two Europeans whom Ruth Awante had seen in the hallway. The heavyset man's name was Lloyd Thurston, an American staying in room 1238, down the hall from Moseley's. Bwana Thurston had not checked out, and, so far as the clerk knew, would be back later that evening. The second man was as much a mystery to him as he had been to the former pickpocket.

This much Andrew learned from Constable Kobari in the Toyota Land Cruiser as they raced along Uhuru Avenue toward the airport, through the gray twilight crouched around the headlamp beams.

In exchange for the information, Andrew related his Jeannette Moseley theory, which Kobari found quite impressive.

Kobari, alas, was quite easily impressed.

"And so now," said Kobari, slamming the stick shift into what seemed like eighth gear, "we go to the airport to pick up the man from the American Embassy?"

"No," said Andrew. "We go to the airport to learn whether either of the two *Wazungu* seen by Ruth Awante is there. The seven thirty plane leaves at eight o'clock to return to Nairobi. It is the last one out tonight."

"One of these men, you think, was Jeannette Moseley." He stared at Andrew.

"The thin one, yes. And please keep your eye on the road."

"But, sergeant." Kobari glanced briefly at the road, satisfied himself that no collision was imminent, and looked back to Andrew. "If he believes he has fooled us with his masquerade, he has no reason to leave the Township tonight. He could leave in perfect safety at any time."

"Perhaps, yes. But why should he remain here? His work is done, and the longer he stays, the greater grows the possibility that he will be found out."

"Ah," said Kobari, and swung the Toyota in a sickening lurch around a large piebald dog whose astonishment at the constable's driving had rendered him paralyzed. "I see." He nodded with conviction.

A conviction which Andrew wished he felt himself. The man might leave tomorrow, or indeed a week or a month from today. He might leave by bus or by train or by rented car. And if he did not attempt the plane tonight, most likely he would never be found, not among the thousands of tourists in the Township.

Particularly since no one but Andrew wished to find him.

Luck would be required here.

As it happened, Andrew's luck appeared to be excellent. First, the plane from Nairobi was late (less luck than inevitability), which meant that Andrew might be able to avoid the embassy person. Second, at seven forty-five, through the swinging glass doors of the terminal came a man with short-cropped blond hair, blue eyes, and glasses, wearing a khaki safari suit, carrying a single large suitcase.

Andrew and Kobari were sitting at the end of a line of orange plastic chairs, each of which had been carefully molded to provide maximum discomfort. Tourists milled about the brightly lit room, chattering and yammering, gesticulating with bottles of Coca-Cola, Happy Time limeade, Tusker Lager.

Andrew saw the man first, turned to Kobari, and said, "There."

Kobari lowered his bottle of limeade and nodded. "You were right, sergeant. Once again, eh?"

"We shall see. Come along."

The two edged through the crowd, which parted to let them pass, people shying away, eyes averted. (In general, tourists had more respect for the local police than the locals did: any black man in uniform might, after all, be a distant cousin of Idi Amin's.) Stepping in front of the man, Andrew said, "Excuse me, sir."

The man turned and looked from him to Kobari, blinking mildly behind his horn-rimmed glasses. "Yes?" He was slender, very trim. Although his skin was large-pored, it was unlined; the features were even, almost delicate. Thin chin, small mouth. His voice was of medium timbre, neither deep nor high. He could, yes, have masqueraded as a woman.

"Sergeant Mbutu, Township Constabulary. This is Constable Kobari. A few questions, sir."

The man's brow furrowed as his glance moved between Andrew and Kobari. "Questions?" he said to Andrew. "About what?" More puzzled than disturbed, and certainly not alarmed.

"Would you step outside of a moment, sir."

"Well, yeah . . . sure." Still puzzled, and still unworried.

Would a typical tourist not react with more alarm to the suggestion that he accompany a pair of policemen out into the African night?

Andrew led the man—and Kobari, who had very professionally fallen behind the suspect—through the doors, across the cement, and into a bright white cone of light beneath a street lamp. Andrew turned to the man and asked, "May I see your passport, please."

"Sure." The man set down the suitcase, reached into the left breast pocket of the safari jacket. Eased out the blue passport, casually handed it to Andrew. "What's this all about, sergeant?" As though merely curious.

Without answering, Andrew opened the passport. Carl Fogarty, Los Angeles, California. Birthdate: March 23, 1956. Thirty-two years old.

Andrew flipped through the pages. The document was new: only one entry stamp. The man had arrived in the country six days ago.

Closing the passport but not handing it back, Andrew looked up at the man and said, "Your first time abroad, Bwana Fogarty?"

Fogarty smiled, showing two rows of teeth too perfect to be real. Rather like the man himself. "That's right, yeah. I always wanted to see Africa." Another toothy smile as he gestured toward the darkness around. "And here I am."

Andrew nodded. "Bwana Fogarty, we have testimony that you were with a Bwana Lloyd Thurston late this afternoon, on the twelfth floor of the Hotel Soroya."

The man blinked again. "Well, yeah. Sure. I was there. What's wrong? Something happen to Thurston?"

Puzzlement again, but no real confusion. Too calm by half.

"Not to Bwana Thurston, no. But there has been a homicide. I would be grateful if you would accompany us to the station to answer some questions."

Fogarty frowned—blandly, mildly—and looked at his wrist watch. "Well, you know, sergeant, I've got this plane to catch. I leave for the States tomorrow, from Nairobi."

"If you are delayed, we will reimburse you for any expenses. And if necessary, we will provide you with accommodations." If necessary, for the rest of your life.

It was as though the man had caught Andrew's thought. For the briefest of moments, so quickly that afterward it might never have happened, something flickered behind the bland, indifferent mask. For an instant, the pale blue eyes flashed with calculation as they darted from Andrew to Kobari.

Got you, you bastard. Andrew felt his muscles tense.

But then the man smiled. Blandly. Indifferently. He shrugged in resignation and said, "Well, all right. If you think it's important."

As the three of them walked toward the Toyota, Kobari asked in Swahili, "Sergeant, what about the plane? The passenger?"

"We'll radio from the car, have the station send someone."

The man's blandness was a wall, solid as rock, impenetrable. Smiling pleasantly, nodding amiably, for over an hour now he had refused to alter the account he had first given Andrew in the Toyota.

Andrew said, "Let us go over this once again, Bwana Fogarty. You arrived in the Township when, exactly?"

"Like I told you, sergeant. Six days ago, on the tenth."

"And you stayed where?"

"At the Aladdin Hotel."

The two of them were sitting in the least unpleasant of the three interrogation rooms at the station, the room used exclusively for tourists.

Few tourists would have considered themselves favored. A single bare light bulb burned overhead; the cement walls and the cement floor were painted a sickly pale green. Built midway into the steel door was a sliding steel observation gate, rusted shut. The only window was a small barred rectangle set near the ceiling, beyond a thicket of spiderwebs.

But instead of a pair of hard wooden benches, the only furniture in the other rooms, this one held two sagging cots, a small wooden table, and two upright wooden chairs. Andrew sat in one, Fogarty in the other. Constable Kobari had been sent off to verify what he could of the man's story.

Andrew said, "And what was it that brought you to the Township?"

"Like I said, I always wanted to see Africa. Just never had the time before, or the money."

"But why this Township in particular?"

Fogarty shrugged. "I heard it was a nice place."

"And how exactly did you obtain the money? And the time?"

Fogarty sighed lightly. "Like I said, I had a good year. Decided it was time to give myself a real vacation."

"And what is your occupation?"

"I own a sporting goods store. In Los Angeles."

"Would such a place offer rifles for sale?"

"Sure. And pistols." Fogarty smiled that mild insufferable smile. "And tents and sleeping bags."

Maddening. Behind his polite inflexible mask, the man was mocking him. Fogarty was guilty, and Andrew knew it, and Fogarty knew that Andrew knew it. But both knew that Andrew might never prove it.

"Do you own a rifle, Bwana Fogarty?"

"I own a lot of rifles, sergeant. I've got maybe forty or fifty in inventory."

"Do you personally own a rifle? Do you keep one in your home?"

"No."

"Have you ever fired a rifle?"

"I told you, sergeant. I'm not into rifles."

"Did you bring a rifle with you when you came to this country?"

"No."

"Did you obtain one when you arrived?"

Another light sigh. "No."

"And when did you meet Bwana Forrest Tupperman?"

"Sergeant, I told you. I *never* met him. I'd never even heard of him till you mentioned his name."

"Explain again how you happened to be on the twelfth floor of the Hotel Soroya."

But at that moment the steel door swung open and Constable Ngio stepped into the room. His eyes shifting, his glance avoiding Andrew's, he said, "The chief wants to see you."

Why was the chief still here, when normally he left the station at seven? Had he waited for the attaché from the American Embassy?

And why had Ngio looked—or rather, not looked—at Andrew so strangely?

Andrew knocked on the office door, heard the chief's voice rumble, "*Karibu.*" Enter.

Andrew opened the door.

The chief sat behind his desk, a big man, taller and broader even than Constable Gona. Sitting opposite him, and swiveled round in his chair to face Andrew, was another big man, nearly the chief's size, a European or an American in a rumpled gray suit. His short wavy hair was the same color as the suit, his broad face was red, the cheeks and nose alight with a fine network of exploded capillaries.

"Come in, sergeant, and sit down," said the chief.

Andrew did so, sitting to the right of the large stranger. Cramped into the same room with these two, he felt like a dwarf.

The chief said, "This is Bwana Emerson, from the American Embassy."

Andrew nodded; the big man nodded back, his face expressionless, and said "Hi ya."

"Bwana Emerson is here to work with us on the investigation of the death of Bwana Tupperman. He would like to talk to you."

Andrew nodded.

"But first," said the chief, "I would like a few words with you myself." The chief turned to the big American. "Bwana, you are welcome to use the room next to this one, on the left. I shall send Sergeant Mbutu over in a moment."

Emerson nodded. "Right." He pulled himself up from the chair—evidently, from the grunt and the unhappy wheeze, no easy task—then lumbered to the door, opened it, and stepped out into the hallway, pulling the door shut behind him.

Andrew turned to the chief, who was watching him carefully.

The chief said, "Cadet Inspector Moi is displeased, sergeant."

"Yes, sir?" So Moi had gone whining to Poppa. No wonder Ngio had acted awkwardly: poor Mbutu's in the soup again. Whole station probably knew about it by now.

Amazingly, annoyingly, Andrew's ears began to burn.

The chief said, "He was in here for about fifteen minutes, storming around in those blue jammies of his."

Andrew ventured a smile, hopeful and flimsy.

The chief did not return it. "He's made some serious charges, sergeant. Apparently he gave you a direct order. To proceed to the airport, locate Bwana Emerson, and return with him to the station. Apparently you disobeyed that order, and brought an American national in for questioning. Can you explain yourself?"

"Yes, sir," Andrew said. "I believe so. By luck, while I was waiting at the airport, I noticed the American. He matched the description of a man who had been seen on the twelfth floor of the Soroya. At approximately the time the shot was fired which killed Bwana Tupperman."

"By luck, is it."

"Yes, sir."

"The thought hadn't occurred to you that he might be there?"

"Well, yes," said Andrew, shifting slightly on his seat. "I did consider it a possibility."

"Has the man admitted that he was there at the Soroya?"

"Yes."

"You brought him in as a witness?"

Andrew hesitated.

The chief nodded. "Moi wasn't altogether coherent, but I gather he feels you think that this man is something more."

Andrew nodded. "I believe he is the assassin."

"Explain."

Andrew related, once again, his theory about Jeannette Moseley.

The chief sat there, immobile, his wide face empty. He could have been staring at the wall. He could have been, himself, the wall stared at. When Andrew had finished, he nodded once, then said, "Do you think, sergeant, that this idea of yours is any less unlikely than Moi's notion of a vengeful secretary?"

"Both are unlikely, sir. Admittedly. But I believe mine to be true."

The chief nodded again. He picked up a letter opener, studied it for a moment; finally, without looking up, he nodded once more. "Twenty-four hours, sergeant."

"Sir?"

The chief looked up. "You can hold this man for twenty-four hours. If in that time you find something to validate your belief, we will proceed. If not, we release him."

"Yes, sir," said Andrew. He added, "Legally, sir, we can hold him without charge for forty-eight hours."

For the first time, the chief smiled. It was a famous smile, lips grim, eyes cold; a smile which, rumor had it, had once caused a visiting minister to cut short his holiday in the Township by a week.

"Thank you, sergeant," he said, his voice rumbling gently, "for apprising me of the law."

Not for the first time, Andrew understood how the minister must have felt.

"The fact is," said the chief, "you have virtually nothing to connect this man to the murder. I'm giving you the twenty-four hours because in the past your judgment has occasionally proved correct. I hope it will prove so once again."

"Yes, sir."

The chief nodded. "All right. Constable Kobari's waiting for you in the dispatcher's office. When you've finished with him, talk to this Emerson fellow. He looks rather like a clown, but I very much suspect he's not. He tells me he used to be a police officer himself, and I believe him."

"Yes, sir," said Andrew and stood.

"Oh, and, sergeant?"

"Sir?"

"I suggest you stay out of Moi's path for a few days."

"The toilet seat," said Emerson, smiling and shaking his head. "I like it. I like it a lot."

From the small bottle he had produced from his jacket pocket, he poured some more whisky into his water glass. He screwed the cap back on and returned the bottle to the pocket. Then, sitting back and holding the glass with both hands—with surprising daintiness, rather like a matron afraid to spill even a drop of sherry—he said, "But a woman could of left the seat up. Specially this babe. I mean, maybe she dumped some evidence in there."

"She would not have needed to lift the seat to do so," Andrew pointed out.

Emerson shrugged. "You say all the prints were wiped away. Maybe she left it up after she cleaned it."

"Perhaps. But between the time the shots were fired and the time the first police officer entered the room, the only people seen in the hallway were the two men, Bwana Thurston and Bwana Fogarty."

Emerson nodded. "You find this Thurston guy yet?"

"No. We are still looking for him."

Emerson nodded again and took a delicate sip of whisky.

The man was completely unlike any of the (very few) embassy people Andrew had met. Those had worn neatly pressed tropical weight suits, crisp off-white shirts, Italian ties, and shoes so highly polished you could see in them the reflection of the sky. Emerson's shoes were scuffed, his shirt and tie spotted with soup stains, and his suit looked as though it had been used to haul rocks.

Now, looking at Andrew over the rim of the glass, he said, "Okay. How much of Fogarty's story checks out?"

"All of it," Andrew told him.

Constable Kobari had so informed him in the dispatcher's office.

Andrew said, "He arrived here six days ago, on the tenth, and checked into the Aladdin Hotel. He kept very much to himself, although he rented a car and made several day trips. To visit Tsavo, he says, and there is no one to contradict him." Tsavo being a game park one hundred kilometers to the west.

Another nod. "When did Jeannette Moseley check into the Soroya?"

"Yesterday. She, too, seems to have kept very much to herself."

"Which doesn't prove anything."

"No," Andrew admitted.

"Moseley, or whoever it was, asked for a room on that side of the hotel? On that floor?"

"Yes. On that side, and for a room on the eleventh or twelfth floor. There was a room available. Most guests prefer a room that faces the sea."

Emerson nodded, then sipped at the whisky. "What about the suitcases? How'd Fogarty work that, you figure?"

"He could have come into the country with both, one containing the Jeannette Mosely identity."

"The brands match?"

"No."

A nod. "What's he tell the guys at customs when they open up the bags?"

"Thousands of tourists come through Nairobi Customs every day. Even if Bwana Fogarty had been one of the very few who are stopped to have their luggage opened, he could have told the examiner that they were clothes for a wife, or for a female acquaintance, who had arrived at an earlier date. By now, no one would remember him."

Emerson nodded. "They remember at the Aladdin how many bags he was carrying when he showed up?"

"They do, yes. One."

A sip of whisky. "Okay. Hypothetically. He comes into town with two bags. He leaves the Moseley bag at a locker in the airport. Those are good for a week, right?"

Andrew nodded.

"He goes to the Aladdin," Emerson continued, "and checks in as Fogarty. Then, yesterday, he rents a car, picks up the bag, and drives somewhere to get into the dress, or whatever. And the wig."

"And put on the brown contact lenses."

"Yeah, right, the contact lenses. Then he parks the car somewhere and goes and checks into the Soroya as Moseley."

"Yes. I believe that this, or something like it, is what he did."

"And then, today, after he shoots Tupperman, he goes back to the Aladdin wearing the Fogarty outfit. He ditches the contacts and the wig somewhere along the way."

"And, I believe, a pair of gloves."

Emerson frowned. "Gloves?"

"We administered a paraffin test to his hands. The results were negative. I believe he wore gloves when he fired the rifle, and then disposed of them with the rest."

"He agree to the paraffin test?"

"Yes. He has been most cooperative."

Emerson smiled and sat back. "If you're right about all this, you got yourself one smart puppy here, sergeant."

Andrew nodded. "I believe he is very clever indeed."

"You also got yourself two major problems."

"Yes?"

"First of all, to check into the Soroya, Moseley had to hand a passport over to the desk clerk. You guys got it?"

"Yes. We obtained it from the hotel. The entry stamp, dated three days ago, is obviously a forgery. But of course, it had to fool only the desk clerk."

"The photo look like Fogarty?"

"There is a resemblance, yes. But by itself, it is not enough to convict him, or even to bring him to trial."

Emerson nodded. "You got any other record of Moseley entering the country? Passenger manifest? Customs card?"

"None."

Emerson nodded. "The passport's a phony."

"Yes. It would not, otherwise, have been left behind."

"Okay. You got another problem."

Andrew nodded. "The weapon, yes."

"Yeah. Fogarty didn't tote that rifle through customs."

"As I see it, there are two possibilities. Either he arranged somehow to have the rifle waiting for him here. Or he drove down to Mombasa and purchased it there on the black market."

"Either way," Emerson said, "you mix that with the phony passport, and you toss in everything else, and you got yourself what looks like a fairly professional shooter."

"I agree."

Emerson sipped at his whisky. "Now why would a professional-type shooter want to blow away a tourist-type guy like Tupperman?"

"I do not know. I was hoping that perhaps you might help us discover the answer."

Emerson raised an eyebrow. "How so?"

"Would it be possible for your embassy to determine something of Mr. Tupperman's background?"

The American shrugged his heavy shoulders. "No sweat. I already called the chief of police in Tarpon Springs. He'll be getting back to me sometime tonight." He sipped at his whisky. "Anything else?"

"Yes." Andrew was on uncertain ground now, and unsure how to proceed. "I should like your opinion as to whether this killing might have been an assassination arranged, perhaps, by some governmental department."

Emerson was smiling. "Yeah? Which government you got in mind?"

"None," said Andrew, and realized that his eyes were blinking rapidly. "None in particular. I was merely wondering what you might think."

Emerson grinned, patently amused. "What're we talking here, sergeant? KGB? CIA?"

Andrew shifted uncomfortably in his seat. "I do not know, of course. I merely put forward—"

Emerson crossed his legs comfortably. "Look, sergeant. I think you can forget that stuff. I don't know much about the KGB, naturally, but I've met a couple of bozos in the CIA. Part of my job. And if the CIA wanted to trash Tupperman, they'd of used some nifty aftershave that maybe, two months from now, turned his nose into a brussels sprout. So he couldn't breathe."

He grinned. "Fiendish, see. They like fiendish. Especially the new ones. They wouldn't of used a sniper rifle." He snorted. "And if they did, they would of missed."

"What is your job, Bwana Emerson? If I may ask."

Emerson tossed back the last of his whisky. "Consultant. Security. Till next week anyway. And then I'm history."

"You are leaving the embassy?"

"Yeah." He grinned. "Why do you think I got sent down here? I'm the only guy around who's expendable."

"You will be returning to the United States?"

Emerson's smile became rueful. "Yeah. Back to Disneyland." He looked down, saw that his glass was empty, frowned, then turned to set it on the small table to his left. He turned to Andrew. "Anyway. Fogarty. What about his story that he got off on the twelfth floor by mistake?"

"It would be possible. The restaurant, for which he claims he was looking, is on the top floor of the Soroya. There are two rows of buttons in the elevator. The first runs from the lobby to the twelfth floor, the second from the thirteenth floor to the restaurant. He maintains that he hit the wrong button by mistake. The twelfth, not the twenty-fourth."

"And then he wandered all the way down to the end of the hallway before he figured out he screwed up?"

"Yes. This, I think, is the weakest part of his story."

"But possible."

Andrew shrugged. "Possible, yes."

"And while he's stumbling around up there, he runs into Thurston."

"Yes. He says they had not met before. He says that he explained his mistake to Thurston, and that Thurston suggested Fogarty accompany him to another restaurant, the Sinbad."

"Your guy check at the Sinbad?"

"Yes. The two of them were seen eating there between five thirty and six, yesterday afternoon. Fogarty says he left at six fifteen and returned to the Aladdin to pack for his departure."

"He still would of had time to dump the stuff. The wig and all."

"Yes. He could have been carrying everything in the pockets of his safari suit."

Emerson pursed his lips. "That maid at the Soroya. She only saw Fogarty when he came down the hall with Thurston."

"That is correct. If he is telling the truth, Ruth Awante somehow missed seeing him when he first came off the elevator."

"And you don't think that happened."

"No."

Emerson looked off for a moment, then looked back at Andrew. "Okay, sergeant. It could of gone down the way you see it." He shrugged his heavy shoulders. "We got a lotta gender benders in the States. Guys dressed up like women. And vice versa. And they do a good job at it, too, some of 'em. So why not a shooter? But if it happened that way, this Fogarty is a real sweetheart. He doesn't make mistakes."

"Except, perhaps, the toilet seat."

Emerson grinned. "Yeah, except that, maybe. But on the other hand, you could have it all wrong. Fogarty could be a civilian who just got caught in the wrong place at the wrong time." He grinned. "But you don't think so, right?"

"I am convinced he is guilty. There is something . . . somehow unreal about him."

"Okay. Look. What's his status at the moment? Is he under arrest, or what?"

"We are holding him without charge. He is, officially, a material witness. Unless we find tangible evidence of his involvement, he will be released tomorrow."

"You guys search him?"

"No."

"Collect his personal effects?"

"We examined his suitcase, and returned it to him. Since he is, at the moment, merely a witness, we have no legal reason to keep it."

Emerson raised his eyebrows. "You guys always such sticklers for detail?"

"He is an American national, and a tourist."

Smiling, Emerson said, "And the tourist business is pretty good these days."

Andrew found himself stiffening slightly. "We operate according to guidelines sent down from Nairobi."

"Hey, I know," Emerson said, grinning now, waving a placatory hand. "Don't get your bowels in an uproar."

He leaned forward slightly. "Okay. Here's the deal. The whole reason I'm here is to protect American interests. Right? So maybe I got to protect Fogarty's. Lemme talk to him. Get a handle on him. Maybe he's a bad guy, maybe he's not. I got to make some kind of determination for myself. You gonna be here for a while?"

"If necessary, yes."

" 'Kay. I'll get back to you."

Emerson returned a half an hour later. Without a word he crossed the room, sat down again in the battered upholstered chair, reached into his jacket pocket, and slipped out the whisky bottle. He unscrewed the cap, poured amber fluid into his water glass, recapped the bottle and returned it to his jacket. He lifted the glass, squinted at it thoughtfully for a moment, took a delicate sip, and sighed. "You're right," he said, and he appeared to be addressing the glass more than he was Andrew. "Guy's not kosher."

"Is there any way," Andrew asked him, "we can obtain information from the United States about Bwana Fogarty?"

Still staring into the glass, Emerson nodded. "I can call the LAPD. See what they got." He turned to Andrew. "Tell you what. Mrs. Tupperman's all doped up right now. Sedatives. But I got to talk to her tomorrow. You wanna come along?"

"The constabulary has already interviewed Mrs. Tupperman."

Emerson frowned at his whisky glass. "That guy Gona?"

"Yes."

"Terrific." He looked over again to Andrew. "How 'bout I arrange it with your chief?"

"Yes," Andrew said. "In that case I should be happy to do so."

Emerson nodded, stared back at his glass. "Good. Guy's not kosher. I wanna nail him."

Andrew and Emerson sat at a round white metal table on the tiled patio of the Soroya Hotel. A warm breeze scudded in off the ocean, leaving feathery whitecaps out there in the blue. It tugged and snapped at the canvas canopy overhead, and carried the tang of salt and the candied scent of suntan oil whisked from the shiny, pink, semi-naked European bodies scattered, shoulder to shoulder, along the sunswept beach.

Emerson, in the same remarkably unremarkable clothes he had worn yesterday, stared glumly out past the casurina pines and across the mosaic of sleek backs and slick bellies. He lifted his glass and took a gulp, not at all delicately, from his bourbon and water. "Ya know," he said, "I was here once before. 'Bout twenny years ago."

Andrew, feeling as glum and discouraged as Emerson looked, was surprised to find within himself, still, a measure of politeness. "Yes?"

Emerson nodded. "Yeah. Stood out there on the beach. Probly just about there, where those German guys are sitting. None of this was here then. The hotel, none of it. I looked up and down and, ya know, all you could see in either direction was the sand and the water and the palm trees. And a couple fishing boats, bringing in the catch. And I remember thinking, Geeze, it'd be okay to die now. Right this minute. And it would of been. I wouldn't of minded at all, not a bit, because right then I'd already been to heaven. . . ." He frowned, took another drink. "Just over there. Where the German guys are."

Slowly, idly, Andrew ran his finger down the mist clouding his glass of limeade. "You were in the armed forces?"

Emerson looked at him. "Huh?"

"We did not have tourists then. Usually only American servicemen."

Out in the surf, a young European girl in a leopard skin bikini squealed with pleasure as a wave smacked against her tanned thigh.

Emerson nodded. "Yeah. The armed forces." He looked out again across the recumbent bodies. "Too many people in the world, sergeant. Way too many." He swallowed some of his drink. "You know about Norway rats?"

"Sorry?" said Andrew. "Norway rats?"

Another nod. "Guy named Calhoun did an experiment with Norway rats. There's always a maximum number of rats in a colony, see. Calhoun stuck more of 'em in there, made all 'em live together. Know what happened?"

"No." And did not especially care to; but realized that he soon would.

"They started killing each other off. Kept at it till the colony got back to normal."

"Ah."

"Won't happen with us, though," Emerson said, still looking off.

"Too many colonies. Past the point of no return. And we're different. We don't just kill each other. We got advantages that the Norway rats don't have. We can kill the ocean. We can kill the atmosphere." He frowned. "We're gonna kill off the whole thing."

"The world, you mean?" Andrew asked.

"Yeah," said Emerson. "The whole ball of wax."

"If you genuinely believe that," Andrew asked him, curious, "why is it so important to you that we prove Fogarty guilty?"

Emerson swallowed some more whisky. "Habit."

Andrew smiled. "I think, Bwana Emerson, that you are perhaps somewhat dispirited this morning."

Emerson turned to him. "Yeah. Somewhat."

So far, truly, it had not been a promising day. Emerson had met Andrew at the station, where the two had begun it by exchanging disappointments.

First, Lloyd Thurston had been apprehended as he returned to the Soroya after spending a long night at the Delight with one of the Somali women. In every particular, he had substantiated Fogarty's story.

Second, Emerson had heard from his sources in the United States. Carl Fogarty had no police record and no known criminal associates. An employee at his Los Angeles shop had informed the local police that he was on vacation in Africa.

Forrest Tupperman, too, had no record and was also on vacation in Africa. This last information had been supplied to the Tarpon Springs police department by his secretary, Gladys Norman, who had never been out of the United States in her life, much to Cadet Inspector Moi's immense disgust.

Third, Mrs. Evelyn Tupperman had no idea at all why anyone might want to kill her husband. A tall gangly woman wrung dry by grief, lost and alone within an ill-fitting green polyester jumpsuit, she could tell Andrew and Emerson nothing that helped. Shown the two passport photos, of Fogarty and Moseley, she had been unable to identify either.

Mr. Tupperman had no enemies. Mr. Tupperman's construction business was doing well. Mr. Tupperman had never been to Africa before.

One fact of possible importance: since they had arrived, ten days before, Mr. Tupperman usually spent the late afternoon sunbathing on the balcony.

After obtaining a photograph of the deceased, Andrew and Emerson had left.

Andrew tasted his limeade: tepid now. He frowned and said, "Do you think it would be worthwhile to wait another day and speak with the wife again?"

Emerson shook his head. "Nah. She doesn't know anything."

"Perhaps she will remember something later. At the moment she is disoriented."

Emerson shrugged. "Yeah, well. Can you blame her? Never been outside the States before. 'Course she's disoriented. Even if her husband hadn't been blown away, she'd still be disoriented." Rather grumpy; still nettled, perhaps, by his Norway rats. "You got a different language here. Different money. Different everything. Street signs, road maps. You don't even number the rooms in the damn *buildings* the same way." He leaned forward and pounded the ball of his fist against the table. "*Damn.* He *did* it. I *know* he did." He shook his head. "Bastard just didn't make any mistakes."

He looked at Andrew. "You know what we're missing here? The big thing?"

Andrew watched a seagull swoop down and scoop something from the choppy surface of the sea. "A motive?"

"Motive, right. Why Tupperman? Why kill a poor schlep like Tupperman? Doesn't make any sense."

Andrew sat abruptly upright. "No," he said. "It does not." Somewhere inside him a possibility had begun to tremble.

Emerson shook his head. "Bastard didn't make any mistakes at all."

Andrew said, "But perhaps he did."

The name Michael Buonarotti meant nothing whatever to Andrew. For Emerson, however, it had an immediate significance, which he explained, at length, before the two of them spoke to the man.

Buonarotti was short and stocky. He wore a blue terry cloth robe opened nearly to the navel, displaying several ornate gold chains which hung down through an ornate thatch of gray fur and trailed against the slope of a powerful globular stomach. His face was globular as well, with small, watchful, globular eyes set between horizontal folds of flesh. He was bald, and, like many bald men, had attempted to compensate for the lack of hair on top by cultivating the crop that grew in front: a bushy gray mustache concealed his upper lip and revealed only the pendulous droop of the lower.

With tinkling, clinking drink in hand—Americans were evidently never without their alcohol—he led Andrew and Emerson into the sitting room. "Have a seat, fellas. What can I do ya for?" Although he was affable enough—indeed, expansive—his eyes never lost their watchfulness.

Andrew and Emerson sat on the couch, Buonarotti in a padded leather chair, his legs crossed. His shins were bare and hairy, his feet loosely encased in flip-flop plastic sandals.

As he and Andrew had earlier agreed, it was Emerson who did the talking. "We were wondering if you heard about the American who got shot yesterday."

Buonarotti nodded. "Yeah, sure. Naturally. Cops all over the place. Terrible thing, huh? A real tragedy." He turned to Andrew, who was busy attempting, as Emerson had suggested, to look menacing. A role he was seldom called upon to play with *Wazungu.* Buonarotti asked, "You guys find out who did it?"

"Maybe," said Emerson. "We got kind of an identity problem."

Buonarotti frowned. "How's that?"

Emerson reached into his jacket pocket, pulled out the two passports Andrew had given him. He held one out to the other American. "You recognize this person?"

Buonarotti set his drink down on the coffee table, took the passport, opened it, studied the photo for a moment. He shook his head, frowning. "Nope. Sorry." He looked at Andrew.

Think *killer,* Emerson had said.

Jack the Ripper.

Absurd, really; but it seemed to work: Buonarotti blinked and looked away. He leaned forward to hand back the document and Emerson took it, his face unreadable. "You're sure?"

"Sure. Positive. What's this all about?" Another glance at Andrew. *Joseph Stalin.*

Emerson handed Buonarotti the other passport. "What about this one?"

Buonarotti opened the passport, looked down at the photo, frowned, looked up at Emerson for a second, then again back down at the photograph. He closed the passport and looked back at Emerson. "This is a joke, right?"

"You recognize that person?"

Buonarotti's glance shifted from Emerson to Andrew (*Adolph Hitler*) and back again. "I want a lawyer. I'm an American citizen. I got rights."

Emerson shook his head. "Nah. What you got, ace, is squat. You're not back on your own turf here. You're out in the boonies. The real boonies." He jerked his thumb toward Andrew. "These boys don't fool around. Make 'em unhappy and, boom, you're landfill. I asked you a question. You know that person or not?"

Buonarotti considerd for a moment. He looked once more at Andrew. (*Double Adolph Hitler.*) At last he said, "What's in it for me?"

Emerson turned to Andrew and smiled. "See? I told you he was a reasonable guy."

At two o'clock that afternoon, Andrew and Emerson entered the interrogation room.

Fogarty, who had spent the night there, sat at the head of one of the cots, back against the wall, feet on the mattress, arms wrapped around drawn-up knees.

Emerson was smiling amiably. "How you doin', Carl? They treatin' you all right?"

Fogarty shrugged. "I don't have any complaints."

"Good, good," Emerson grinned. "Glad to hear it. Listen, you mind if we join you for a while? The sergeant here wants to shoot the breeze a bit."

Fogarty produced the familiar mild smile. "Do I have any choice?"

"Not a one, Carl," Emerson beamed. "We'll just park ourselves over here," indicating the other cot. As he and Andrew sat, he said, "You go ahead, sergeant. It's your movie."

Andrew looked for a moment at Fogarty, the bland unworried features, the blue eyes calm behind the horn-rimmed glasses, and he felt a flicker of what might, in some other context, almost be admiration. And then he said, "The difficulty from the beginning, was that you seemed to have made no mistakes. There was no real evidence to link you to the killing of Bwana Tupperman. There was not even, or so it seemed, any motive for the crime."

Fogarty smiled. "Because I didn't kill him."

"Oh, yes," said Andrew. "You did, of course. Because there *was* a motive, and you *did* make a mistake. A most fundamental mistake."

Fogarty said nothing. Merely sat there, still apparently indifferent.

Andrew said, "Bwana Emerson has explained to me that in the United States, the floors of a building are numbered differently from the way they are here. What we call the ground floor, you call the first. What we call the first floor, you call the second. And what we call the eleventh floor, you call the twelfth. Yesterday, it was your intention to kill the occupant of room 1256 of the Hotel Jasmine. From your own room at the Soroya, you counted floors from the ground floor up, to the floor you *believed* to be the twelfth. And there, within your sights, was the man you believed to be your target."

Fogarty glanced at Emerson, frowning slightly.

Emerson grinned. "Pretty good stuff, huh, Carl?"

Andrew said, "And that was your mistake. The man you shot was the occupant of room 1156, a man who bore a passing resemblance, particularly at a distance, to the man you actually wished to kill."

Fogarty said to Emerson, "This is crazy."

Grinning, Emerson held up a hand. "Trust me, Carl. It gets better."

"It was a particularly stupid mistake," said Andrew. "In order to prepare your story about getting off on the wrong floor of the Soroya, you must have looked directly at the numbered buttons in the elevator. And still you did not notice that in this country there is a ground floor *and* a first floor."

Grinning once again, Emerson said, "I stood up for ya, Carl. Told him it was a mistake any good ole American boy could make."

Fogarty said nothing. But the bland mask was beginning now to slip: the lips had tightened, the blue eyes had narrowed.

Andrew asked him, "Did you know, yesterday, even before you reached the airport, that you had shot the wrong man? Or was it something you learned only when I questioned you?"

Still Fogarty said nothing.

Emerson asked pleasantly, "Cat got your tongue, Carl?"

"We spoke today," said Andrew, "with Michael Buonarotti, the occupant of room 1256 at the Jasmine. As Bwana Emerson has explained to me, Buonarotti is a representative of organized crime in your country. It was he you were supposed to assassinate. And it was he who has identified you. Apparently you have something of a reputation in those circles."

Andrew stood. "And now, I am afraid, we must end this." He walked over to the steel door and pulled it open. Waiting in the hallway were Constable Satyit, one of the prison matrons, and Sister Margaret, a nurse from Uhuru Hospital. Both of them, by their size, might have been sisters to Constable Gona.

Andrew ushered them in.

Fogarty looked at the women, looked back at Andrew. "What's this?"

"You are under arrest," Andrew said, "and you must be searched. By law, I am not allowed to be present. Only a matron may search a woman."

It was at this point that Fogarty, in effect, surrendered. She let out a deep breath as her shoulders slumped forward, loose and limp.

"But what of the toilet seat?" asked Constable Kobari the next day as they drove along the sea road in the Land Cruiser, palm trees flashing by the open windows. The wind had died overnight; the sea was as flat now as a lake. On the right, out there toward the horizon, a large dhow—carrying mangrove poles for the Saudis, probably—edged slowly northward under engine power, her sails slack. "The toilet seat was up."

Andrew said, "Perhaps, as Bwana Emerson first suggested, she left it up herself, after she wiped away the prints. Or perhaps someone else did."

"But who?"

Andrew shrugged. "I do not know." He could never know, not for certain; but he could, and would, offer prayers to the Gods of Evidence that Constable Gona never again be the first police officer at a crime scene.

"What will happen to her, sergeant?"

"She will be convicted. We have the deposition from Buonarotti, identifying her under her real name." Jeanne LaSalle. "And we have the testimony of Ruth Awante and the desk clerk." Both of whom, confronted with the LaSalle woman in a dress, had identified her as Jeannette Moseley.

"And what of the real Carl Fogarty? In the United States?"

"I imagine that Bwana Emerson is right. That Fogarty was prevailed upon, by LaSalle or by one of her associates, to disappear for a while."

"And his passport?"

"Presumably, Fogarty provided the documentation, and LaSalle the photograph. According to Bwana Emerson, so long as this was Fogarty's first passport, there would have been no difficulty. Bwana Emerson has notified the authorities, and Fogarty will be dealt with. Please keep your eyes on the road."

Kobari looked back at the road and shook his head. "A woman assassin. Who would have thought."

"Women's Liberation," Andrew said. "Apparently, it extends in the United States to every occupation. A most formidable movement."

Kobari frowned. "Why do you suppose Buonarotti was to be assassinated?"

"Who can say? He offended someone, obviously. We shall never know how, I imagine, nor whom. But if I were he, I should be extremely careful when I returned to the United States."

Kobari looked at him. "Do you believe they will try again?"

Missing her by only centimeters, the car raced past a shuffling old woman with a wicker basket atop her head. Her screech died off behind them as the Toyota hurtled toward the Township.

Andrew opened his eyes again. Carefully, precisely, he said, "Slow down the car."

Kobari eased up slightly on the gas. "Do you think they will, sergeant? Try again?"

Andrew took a deep breath. "Probably. Yes. And I should imagine that this time they will select someone for the job who is not quite so clever."

"She wasn't so clever," said Kobari, and smiled. "After all, she couldn't count."

Two months later they, whoever they were, did try again; and this time, using the relatively unclever technique of a hand grenade hurled through the window of Buonarotti's Mercedes, they succeeded.

This Andrew learned from the newspaper clipping sent to him from the United States by Emerson.

There was also a typed note in the envelope:

Thought you might like to see this. Story on the street is that B. was skimming cash off the corporate accounts.

Enjoyed working with you. And enjoyed the drink before I left—you feeling any better? It was good to be back there, and good to help out. Sometimes even a Norway rat gets a chance at atonement. If you're ever in the States, give me a jingle.

At the bottom, an address and a phone number, but no signature.

Andrew handed the note to Kobari, who sat perched on the edge of Andrew's desk at the station. Kobari read it through, handed it back.

He looked puzzled. "What does he mean by atonement?"

"I have no idea."

"He has been here before? In the Township?"

"Twenty years ago, he said."

"So in 1968."

"Very good," Andrew nodded. "Keep up with your arithmetic, and you shall soon be chief."

"That was the year Abbu Messin was killed." Kobari was the station's historian, having memorized every important event in the Township since the Pleistocene.

"Abbu Messin?" Andrew said.

"You don't remember, sergeant?"

Andrew frowned. "Kobari. I was ten years old."

Kobari nodded. "He was a terrorist. Very bad. Even Al Fatah had denounced him, and he was living here in exile. He had a house over by the Salem ginnery. The house burned down, with him in it. A very big affair, very much publicity."

"Who did it?"

"No one knows. People said the CIA, but they always say that. It was never proved."

Andrew nodded.

Kobari said, "Are you ready for lunch?"

"You go ahead," Andrew told him. "I'll meet you at Abdullah's."

After the constable left, Andrew picked up the envelope in which the clipping and the note had come. There was no return address, but the postmark on the front said "Langley, VA."

VA? Virginia?

Langley, Virginia, was the headquarters of the CIA.

No, Andrew told himself. It could not be.

And then he realized: Yes. Of course it could.

Evolution of a Character

Walter Satterthwait's periodic use of variations on Dashiell Hammett's creation, the anonymous Continental Op, is both a complimentary nod to Hammett and a homage to the classic detectives in general. It also makes good use of a character type employed by many writers, actors, traders, and other con men: the deceptively dowdy, rumpled, small, jovial, apparently simple, unintimidating fellow who looks perfectly harmless but in reality is about to eat your lunch. This character, exemplified by the television sleuth Columbo, is meant to be underestimated. He is supposed to look and act like someone a few sandwiches short of a picnic who is no threat to anyone. The bumbling, shabby, confused fool dates back to Greek and Roman drama, was used as comic relief in Shakespeare, and was a staple in Commedia del Arte. I'm not sure when this basic character stopped being a sidekick and moved from the Sancho Panza role to center stage, but Hammett, one of the most literary of genre writers, employed his short, fat detective in a distinctive series of short stories in the period between the wars. For Hammett the fellow was a sort of alter ego, in direct contrast to the dapper, slender, tall, handsome socialite in *The Thin Man* and other novels.

In Satterthwait's work the seedy detective is a deliberate homage to one of his literary heroes and a useful character in his own right. The gumshoe appears full blown in the following story from 1984 as Albuquerque private eye Phil Grober, who reappears later as Joshua Croft's backup in *At Ease with the Dead,* relocated to El Paso. The Continental Op type also appears centrally in *Miss Lizzie* and the African short story "Make No Mistake." But it is Grober in "A Matter of Pride" who most perfectly exemplifies the type. From the moment he wakes up badly beaten in a Santa Fe alley until very nearly the end of the story, he is such a perfect picture of a loser it is obvious why he was chosen by the villain.

This is actually a variation of a classic plot. I remember a story I read in grade school about an apparently weak young private who is given a message and sent on an impossible mission through enemy lines during the European War. He gets captured, of course, but resists an endless nightmare of horrible torture, believing thousands of young soldiers' lives depend on his bravery. He is eventually liberated and brought before his commanding officer, who ruefully admits that he had been given false information and sent on the mission because he was considered most likely to spill his guts and the misinformation would send the enemy on a wild goose chase. His incredible bravery has spoiled the whole operation. Nice twist on the theme of things not being what they appear.

Much of the seedy detective's success is based on the fact that villains, police, relatives, and witnesses all underestimate the short, fat guy with food on the front of his shirt and dandruff on his collar. Grober, whose name is even offensive, simply capitalizes on people's stereotypical assumptions. But, in true Satterthwait fashion, the story is not all that simple, nor the implications so clear-cut as the Op would have found them in the thirties.

The character is intelligent, resourceful, plenty tough, and as thoroughly delightful as Harry Boyle in *Miss Lizzie.* Harry Boyle is also a real Pinkerton man. Here he is described by the novel's narrator Amanda after she airs the opinion that a Pinkerton man should look like a cross between Sherlock Holmes and Buffalo Bill:

> He should not look like a short, overweight, middle-aged former prizefighter. He should not be balding. He should not have, shadowing his jowly cheeks, at least two days' worth of salt-and-pepper stubble. He should not be wearing a brown

suit (even I knew that brown suits were worn only on hayrides), especially one that appeared to have been slept in, frequently, and by several insominacs at once.

Phil Grober is somewhat less endearing in the short story "A Matter of Pride," but his parentage is never in doubt. Here is the Continental Op at his most effective, the seasoned detective who is badly underestimated. Grober, unlike the Op, has no organization to fall back on, though he does have a brother in law enforcement. And while he's sharp enough to work out the crime, he's sloppy enough to be taken in in the first place. The short, fat, seedy detective with a rattletrap car and not enough clients, but with integrity intact. How ironic that the worst punishment Grober can devise for the villain, a hoity-toity nouveau riche art collector posing as a person of class, is loss of face in Santa Fe society. Revenge is made doubly sweet, however, by coming on the heels of the line, "Whose word do you think the police will accept? *Mine,* or that of some fat, sleazy detective?" But this is also one of those twisted tales with at least two victims and two villains, and featuring a type of victim the author is fond of using who rather deserves what he gets at the hands of someone who is likewise unpleasant and hard to empathize with. Justice can then be served in a somewhat skewed way, and literal good and evil are, once again, rather cloudy concepts. The real problem is for Grober himself to save face and get some measure of revenge for having been used.

The story is early enough that Satterthwait disguises the names of bars and restaurants—the Pink Adobe becomes the Purple Hogan, and Satterthwait's old bartending haunt, Vanessie's, is called Victor's. The town of Madrid gets renamed Coreyville. Santa Fe retains its own identity, however, and is virtually a character in the story, so distinctive is its social and economic makeup. Where else, for example, is a crime more likely to be committed over an old Hopi artifact and avenged by loss of face rather than over hunks of money and a drug deal gone sour?

When Grober surfaces again in *At Ease with the Dead* he has slipped back to the level of comic relief and become a caricature of himself:

> Grober was in his mid-forties. About five feet ten, he was stocky and seemed soft and sloppy, but I've seen him take a punch to the gut, one that would turn a weightlifter green, and merely grin. He grew his graying hair long on the left and combed it over the bald spot on top. . . . His face was square, his nose had been broken at least once. He wore a plaid sportscoat, a white shirt, gray Sansabelt slacks, white socks, and spiffy white loafers with leather tassels. He looked like an overnourished, underemployed golf pro.

Grober is professional enough to get the job done for Croft, and even show his tough side in a fight, but he's something of a buffoon. All the same, I expect we'll see other incarnations of the Continental Op.

A matter of Pride

You know it's going to be a bad day when you wake up, face down, in an alley.

It took Grober a while, however, to realize where he was. When he opened grainy eyes to the muddled light of dawn, his mind was suddenly very busy contending with a truly spectacular interior display: little parachutes of pain were opening at the top of his head and fluttering down through his brain, their canopies trembling against his temples and against his jaws before they landed with a startling thud at the base of his skull.

He pushed himself to his knees, felt suddenly sick, and waited there a moment, breathing deeply through an opened mouth. Then, slowly, he sat down in the dirt. He looked around him.

A battered green dumpster; a narrow wooden gate, closed; brown adobe walls on either side. He recognized the place: the alley behind the Purple Hogan, the Santa Fe bar to which, last night, he had tailed Hubbard Baylor.

He shook his head, trying to clear it. A big mistake—the parachutes became packing crates. Teeth grinding, he reached up and felt, gently, the top of his head. And found a long narrow lump, tender and aflame.

This was all beginning to make a kind of dreadful sense. With the chill of certain and irrevocable disaster settling over him, he moved his hand to his back pocket, pushed aside his blue windbreaker, and felt for his wallet. . . .

Danny was sitting back in his office chair reading a copy of *Soldier of Fortune* magazine, his snakeskin boots perched atop his desk. He was wearing fawn-colored slacks, a pale blue shirt, a bolo tie, and a suede sport coat that looked soft enough to spread on bread. Danny dressed exactly like what he was, a Western Lawman: in his case, a lieutenant in the Violent Crimes Unit of the Santa Fe Police Department. No one could have guessed that he, like Grober, had been born and raised in New York City.

"I see by your outfit," said Grober, "that you are a cowboy."

Glancing up from the magazine, Danny said, "You look terrific."

"Thanks," Grober said, closing the door to the squad room.

"You're losing about a pint of blood through each eye."

"I had a rough night. Mind if I sit down?"

Danny shrugged. "The chair belongs to the city. Who am I to say no?" As Grober sat, Danny said, "Instead of drinking, you ever considered just sticking your thumbs into your eyeballs when you get up in the morning? Save you a lot of money on bar bills and give you the same effect."

"I wasn't drinking," Grober said, stretching the truth a bit for drama's sake. "I was sapped and rolled last night."

"Oh yeah?" said Danny, looking down, turning a page of the magazine. "Some twelve-year-old runaway take a dislike to you?"

"It happened here in Santa Fe. You want to hear about it or not?"

Danny studied the magazine. "Sergeant Martinez, outside, can fill out the report."

"Sergeant Martinez isn't my brother."

"No," Danny said, flipping another page. "No such luck."

Grober waited. Finally, Danny sighed. He closed the magazine, tossed it to his desk top, and swung his legs to the floor. "Where'd it happen?"

"The Purple Hogan."

Danny raised an eyebrow. "Pretty upscale place for a mugging."

"In the alley, outside."

Danny nodded. "That sounds more like your style. What time?"

"Around one this morning."

"See the perp?"

"Perp," Grober said. "Nifty. That's police talk, right?"

"Yes or no."

"No."

"Rolled, you said. What'd they get?"

"Everything. Wallet, car keys. My gun."

"That stupid little Baur? You haven't got a permit for that thing, Phil."

"I don't need a permit in New Mexico."

"Only if the weapon is in plain sight."

"I had it Scotch-taped to my forehead. Look, Danny, I'm not in a wonderful mood this morning. I've got a knot on my skull the size of a beef burrito, I've been robbed, they got all my money, they got my car—"

"Your car?"

"—so I'm not really ready to hear you read statutes at me. Yeah, my car."

"Where was it parked?"

"In the lot around the corner."

"How'd they know which car would fit the keys they stole?"

"I don't know. I've been wondering about it myself." He shrugged. "Maybe they tried the keys on every car in the lot until they came to mine."

Danny frowned. "That doesn't play too well. How'd they know the car was in the lot?"

"I don't know."

"Someone bops a guy, rolls him, he's not going to hang around diddling with a bunch of cars."

"I said I don't know."

"Were you working?"

"Yeah. Tailing a guy."

"What guy?"

Grober shook his head. "He didn't do it."

"The name."

Grober smiled. "Or what? Rubber hose time, Danny?"

Danny made a face. "You've got some nerve, Phil. You come in here, you want special attention, Sergeant Martinez isn't good enough for you, but I ask you for a little simple cooperation and you clam up on me."

"I give you the guy, I blow the investigation."

"*Investigation?*" Danny snorted; he was good at snorting. "Who're you, Philo Vance? Some wife wants eight-by-tens of her husband and the chippy he's been jumping, so she can shaft him in court. That's an investigation?"

"One thing you could do, you know. I mean, I can see you're busy and all, but you *could* put my car on the list before some booster's mechanic hacks it up and carts it to Juarez."

Danny laughed. "Yeah. Yeah, right, Phil. There's this terrifically hot market for '72 Pintos in Mexico."

Grober nodded. "I'm glad I could bring a little fun into your life, Danny."

"They're a real prestige item down there. Especially the kind like yours, with that classy coat hanger antenna. Executive-style."

"Maybe you were right. Maybe I should've talked to Sergeant Martinez."

"I think he's already got a Pinto," Danny said, and laughed again.

The telephone on Danny's desk rang. Still grinning, Danny leaned forward and picked up the receiver. "Lieutenant Grober," he said, sitting back in his chair. "Yeah . . . yeah . . . Is that right?" He looked quickly up at Grober. "Yeah, I know where—right here in my office. Thanks, Ed. Appreciate it."

He hung up. "That was Sergeant Munsen," he said. "A couple of uniforms found your car. The DMV got your name from the tags."

Surprised, Grober said, "Where was it?"

"A few blocks from the Purple Hogan. Some kid spotted it and told his mother."

"His mother? Why? Is the car okay?"

"It's not the car so much. It's what was inside."

Grober felt a flutter of unease. "What was that?"

"A stiff. Shot twice in the forehead. A Baur .25 was on the passenger's seat. According to his papers, it was a guy named Baylor. Ring any bells?"

"Oh great," Grober said, slumping back in his chair. "That is just peachy."

"Wouldn't be the guy you were tailing, would it?"

Grober's headache had returned. He rubbed his temples with his fingertips.

"Just peachy."

"Maybe you better tell me about this case of yours."

Grober nodded. "Maybe I better."

She had come into Grober's office yesterday, tall and dark, capped with a helmet of black hair, full breasted but lean as a whippet. She was wearing leather sandals, a flouncy ruffled peasant skirt, several pounds of Navaho silver, and a Danskin top so tight that one good deep breath would have given her thread poisoning. Right hand wielding a brown cigarette, left resting atop the large brown leather bag slung from her shoulder, she looked around Grober's office with airy distaste and turned to him and said, "Are you Mr. Grober?" From her voice, she had gone to one of those Eastern colleges that teach women how to wear tweeds and talk with their teeth clenched.

Belatedly remembering to stand, Grober said, "Yes."

"I'm Winnifred Gail." She said the name as though she were granting a boon.

"Yes?" said Grober.

"The Gail Gallery. In Santa Fe."

"Oh, right," said Grober, who had never heard of the place. "Sure. What brings you to Albuquerque, Miss Gail?"

"Miz."

"Right. Miz." He smiled again, but wondered exactly how big a pain in the neck this woman was likely to be.

"I'm looking for a private investigator."

"Well," he said, smiling his heartiest smile, "it looks like you found one. Have a seat."

She inspected the client's chair for a moment as though she might find some crispy creature lounging on the Naugahyde, then sat down, settling her purse in her lap, crossing her long legs beneath the peasant skirt. She leaned forward and tapped her cigarette against the ashtray on Grober's desk. Her fingernails were long and sharp, painted the color of arterial blood.

Grober sat. "So. What can I do for you."

She inhaled on her cigarette. "I'd like you to locate a man for me."

Grober said, smiling again, "You have a particular man in mind?"

She smiled at him, briefly, bleakly. "Under different circumstances, Mr. Grober, I'm sure I'd find your puckish sense of humor infinitely entertaining. But at the moment, as it happens, I'm in something of a hurry. So suppose we just take my amusement as given, shall we, and dispense with the wit. Yes, a particular man. His name is Hubbard Baylor. Shall I spell that for you?"

A very major pain in the neck, it looked like; but business had been slow lately. Grober picked up his Erasermate. "Two b's in Hubbard?"

She nodded; Grober wrote the name down on his legal pad. He said, "Last known address?"

She gave it, an expensive subdivision on Santa Fe's west side.

"Description?"

"I've a photograph." She rummaged through her purse, found the photograph, held it out. Grober stood up and reached across the desk. "That was taken last week," she said.

It showed two people standing at poolside, arms around each other's waists, both smiling at the camera: Winnifred Gail in a bikini that could fit into an egg cup, and a tall, extravagantly muscled man in a brief swimsuit that could fit into another. His blond hair was artfully tousled, his grin was crowded with shiny teeth, and his heavy jaw looked strong enough to plow a furrow across the state of Indiana.

"He keeps in shape," Grober frowned.

"He works out with weights."

"Swell."

"I should warn you," she said, "that he can be rather a violent man. I've seen him fly into a rage over virtually nothing."

Grober reminded himself to load the Baur. If it came to rage-time, a few .25 slugs in the pecs might slow this bozo down a bit. "Why is it you want to locate him, Ms. Gail?"

Her lips compressed. "I'm not entirely sure," she said, "that that's any of your business." She leaned forward and stabbed her cigarette out in Grober's ashtray.

Grober sighed. "Ms. Gail, I've got a license to think about here. If I'm going to run a trace on somebody, I've got to have a reason, or I could be open to a charge of violating his privacy."

"He stole something from me," she said simply.

"What?"

"A particular piece of art."

"Bigger than a breadbox? Look, you probably want it back, whatever it is. And unless you give me some idea what we're talking about, I could be tripping over the thing all day and never know it."

"I don't want you to approach Hubbard," she said. "Not at all. If you find him, I want you to report to me immediately."

"I don't have any problems with that." He glanced down at the photograph on his desk. The man's bicep was a shade larger than Grober's thigh. "But I'd still like to know what he took."

She frowned. "You're an awfully inquisitive man, Mr. Grober."

"Yeah. In a private detective, that's what you call a selling point."

Her eyes narrowed for a moment, considering; then she said, "Do you know anything about Hopi art?"

"I used to," he said. "But it's all slipped away. Why don't you refresh my memory."

"At the moment," she said, "Hopi art is selling extraordinarily well. Not so much the modern stuff, although that's not doing badly, but the antiquities, pottery and ceremonial objects from Awatovi, the ancestral Hopi city. Three months ago an Awatovi bowl sold in Munich for forty thousand dollars."

"Wait a minute," Grober said. "One bowl? Forty thousand dollars?"

She smiled, amused. "These pieces are appreciating now at an annual rate of over fifty percent, Mr. Grober. They're an excellent investment opportunity."

"Uh-huh. I guess I better tell my broker to dump the AT&T. Okay, so he stole one of these bowls?"

She shook her head. "A *talaotsumsime*."

"Oh. Right. And what would that be?"

"A small stick figure, carved from cottonwood root. It represents one of the Hopi deities, and dates back to the thirteenth century."

"And what's it worth?"

"I'd been offered thirty thousand."

Grober nodded. Forty thousand for a bowl, why not thirty thousand for a bundle of sticks. Clearly, he was in the wrong business. "Did you go to the cops?"

"No."

"How come?"

"For one thing, the provenance of the piece, the history of ownership, is . . . well, I suppose you could call it a trifle murky. The piece is quite genuine—I've had it authenticated—and, naturally, the manner in which I obtained it was perfectly legitimate. But there appear to be a few niggling questions about the manner in which it was originally obtained."

"It's hot, you mean."

"No. I do not mean."

"Warm?"

"I said, merely, that a few questions existed, nothing important, certainly nothing illegal. But there's been quite a lot of controversy recently about the market in Hopi ceremonials. I thought it best to move with discretion in my purchase of the piece, and in the arrangements for subsequent sale. Except for the man from whom I bought it, the man who appraised it, and the client to whom I promised it, only Hubbard knew I had it in my possession."

"And you want to keep it that way."

"Exactly."

"You're sure Baylor stole it?"

"I'm positive. Two days ago. Monday night."

"And he disappeared right afterward?"

"Yes. I tried calling him at his house, but there was no answer. When I drove over, his car was gone. I've made enquiries, discreetly, but no one seems to know where he's gone."

"Could he sell the thing?"

"Certainly. But Hubbard's a collector, it's more likely he plans to keep it. He's independently wealthy, and hardly needs the money he'd obtain."

"You don't have any idea where he could be?"

"None. But he does have a friend in Coreyville, a woman. An old flame of sorts, apparently. They keep in touch, Hubbard told me, and she might know."

"Name and address?"

"Bonnie Little. She runs a restaurant there, I understand, on Main Street." She smiled. "It's called Little's Vittles, if you can believe that. She lives above it."

"Why not just call her up and ask her where he is?"

"If Hubbard has spoken to her, I'm sure he's told her not to discuss anything about him with me."

Grober nodded.

"Incidentally," she said, "I think it would be wise not to mention to the Little woman that you're a private investigator. I don't know how Hubbard would react if he learned of it. Perhaps with violence, perhaps by hiding himself still more deeply. You might tell her that you're an old friend of his—he has a host of colorful characters in his background. You could use that photograph to establish your bona fides, so to speak."

Grober nodded absently; he was trying to picture himself as a colorful character.

"Is there anything else you need to know?" she asked him.

"A few more things," he said. "But first, I'm a little curious about why you didn't go to a Santa Fe PI. Why come down here to me?"

She smiled. "Santa Fe's a small town, Mr. Grober. I'd rather no one there learned that Hubbard has done this to me. A matter of pride, more than anything else."

Grober nodded.

He opened the bottom desk drawer and reached in for a contract. He always had the clients sign a contract; it didn't necessarily keep them, or him, honest; but it kept everyone more or less legal.

She said, "I imagine you'll want a retainer of some sort. What would be reasonable?"

Taking a chance, Grober added fifty dollars to his daily rate, one hundred, and doubled it.

She agreed.

A mining town until its coal seam dwindled away, a ghost town for forty years afterward, Coreyville had become an artists' colony in the early seventies when a group of sculptors and weavers and painters had purchased land at cut-rate prices. Since then, speculators had moved in, and now, if you wanted to describe yourself as a Coreyville artist, you could pay thirty-five thousand dollars for a clapboard house with no plumbing that had, at the turn of the century, cost three dollars and fifty cents. And wasn't, in Grober's opinion, worth that much then or now.

It was an ugly town, locked between drab conical hills spotted with drab conical junipers. The frame houses, all huddled tightly together, still seemed coated with coal dust and soot.

Signs of progress, however, were available. There were boutiques that displayed Navaho pottery crafted by artisans from Newark, New Jersey, who had read extensively about the Navahos. There was a Wild West saloon that offered Japanese beer. There were eateries that supplied food— *quiche, sushi, pasta al pesto*—that would have made the long-departed miners scratch their heads, at prices that would have made them roll in merriment across the quaint hardwood floors.

Little's Vittles was such a place. A small room, low-ceilinged, it held about ten tables, atop each of which was a white tablecloth and an unlit candle in a red glass bowl. Only three of the tables were occupied when

Grober arrived at one thirty that afternoon. He chose the first table by the door, sat down, and examined the menu.

The woman who came to take his order was in her mid-twenties, petite, fine-boned, and wore straight blonde hair down past her shoulders. She also wore a plaid cotton shirt, big denim overalls, a plain white apron, and workboots. Grober was not favorably impressed; in his opinion, bib overalls should be worn only by people named Elmer.

Using his cowboy accent—he was, after all, working undercover—he ordered the teriyaki burger. (Six ninety-five, but it came with organic french fries.) When he finished eating, and the woman returned with his check, he said to her, " 'Scuse me, ma'am, but your name wouldn't be Bonnie Little, now would it?"

She smiled the way people do when a stranger knows their name, with a blend of puzzlement and pleasure. "Yes. But how . . ."

Grober grinned. "Friend of mine up to Santa Fe, Hubbard Baylor, he told me if I ever passed through Coreyville, I ought to stop by, grab some grub, and look you up."

The puzzlement vanished from the smile, leaving only the pleasure. "Do you know Hubbard well?"

"Shoot yes, ma'am. Hub and I go back to the Flood."

The puzzlement returned, her eyebrows knitting. "Hub?"

Grober chuckled uneasily. "Well, yeah, that's what we used to call him down at the gym. Didn't ole Hub never tell you?"

She shook her head, smiling again. "And your name is . . ."

"Billy Bob Gibson, ma'am. No relation to Hoot." Chuckling genially now, Grober stood. "Right pleased to meet you."

"I'm pleased to meet *you*, Mr. Gibson." She offered her hand.

"*Billy Bob*," said Grober expansively, warming to his role. "*Billy Bob*. Don't nobody call me Mr. Gibson, although there's a few owlhoots call me a hell of a lot worse. 'Scuse my language now."

She laughed. "Are you in Coreyville on business, Billy Bob?"

"Nope, thing of it is, I'm on my way to Albuquerque to take a look-see at a passel of fillies for sale down there. Thought I'd stop in, give my hellos. Say now, come to think, you heard anything from ole Hub lately? He plumb dropped outta sight."

She frowned. "But . . ." Her frown deepened.

Grober laughed, knowing that somehow he'd made a mistake, trying to bury it beneath a flood of heartiness. "Now ain't that just like ole Hub?"

She was frowning still, looking at him uncertainly. "Are you sure," she said, "that you're a friend of Hubbard's?"

"Well, course I am, ma'am. Lemme show you." Grateful for the opportunity to establish his bona fides, he tugged his wallet from his back pocket, took from it the photograph given him by Winnifred Gail, handed it to her. "Snapped that last week out to my place. That Hub, he takes a good picture, now don't he?"

"Last week," she said, looking up.

"Yep. Gave a little barbecue, had a few folks over. Roasted an ox."

She frowned again, quickly, sharply, and handed back the photograph. She said, "I'm sorry, Mr. Gibson, but I can't help you."

"How's that," he said, sliding the wallet into his pocket.

"I don't know where Hubbard is."

She was distant now, and cold, and Grober didn't know why.

"Well now," he began.

"I'm sorry," she snapped. "I can't help you. Your bill comes to seven fifty, Mr. Gibson. Will that be cash or charge?"

Time to bail out. "Cash, I reckon."

Grober walked down to the lot where he'd parked the Pinto, got into it, started it, and drove it slowly back toward the restaurant. He parked across the street—in the shade, where, from the restaurant, she would be unlikely to see him inside the car.

Something had put a burr under her saddle. (Remnants of Billy Bob were still coloring Grober's thought.) What had it been? The picture? But she'd been suspicious, closing up, even before she saw it.

He reached over, popped open the glove compartment, took out the pint of V.O., uncapped it, and had himself a hit. He settled back and began to wait. A car passed him, heading south, toward Albuquerque.

At three o'clock, after the restaurant's last customers had left, Bonnie Little hung a CLOSED sign on the window, then crossed the room and disappeared behind the swinging doors that led to the kitchen.

Time passed, and with it some more cars, most of them heading north, toward Santa Fe. Up the street, a motorcyclist in a leather jacket and a white helmet emerged from an alley, climbed aboard a big multi-cylindered Honda, revved it up, and set off for Albuquerque, racing past Grober with a roar.

Idiot, Grober thought. He lifted the bottle of V.O., stopped himself . . . something about the motorcyclist.

Damn. It had been a woman. And bulky jeans, leather workboots. Bonnie Little?

He pulled himself from the car, stalked across the street, pounded at the restaurant's door.

The Hispanic cook, when he finally came, told Grober that Bonnie Little had just left, on her motorcycle.

Grober walked back to the car. He had blown it—she must have spotted him. And there was no way the Pinto could catch up to her machine. The only thing he could do now was wait.

Grober got a big kick out of Cyril Draper. Cyril was something called an amateur sleuth, and he was forever going on vacations to tiny English villages where, between sets of tennis and bridge, he invariably stumbled into a murder investigation. His current investigation concerned the mysterious death (cyanide, bonbons) of Lord Harcourt of Lower Rumple. Cyril had just gathered all the suspects together in the Harcourts' library— Colonel Pottering; Dr. Llewelyn, the vicar; Gwendolyn Montrose; Teddy Semple-Smythe; Naomi Withers (Grober's bet); and Lady Harcourt herself—when the sleek silver Porsche pulled up in front of Bonnie Little's restaurant.

Grober set aside the book (*Death Gets Knocked Up at Nine*) and watched. It was now six o'clock.

Hubbard Baylor stepped from the car. Wearing running shoes, tan slacks, and a white shirt with a little alligator over the heart, he moved smoothly on the balls of his feet, broad shoulders back, lean hips thrust forward, and Grober decided that he, personally, wouldn't want to go up against the man with anything less than a battle cruiser.

Baylor tried the restaurant's door, found it locked, and with no hesitation, reached into his pocket and pulled out a key.

Interesting, Grober thought.

Baylor walked across to the swinging doors, pushed his way through them. Five minutes passed. Then Baylor reappeared through the doors, recrossed the room, left the restaurant, and padded back to the Porsche. He started it and drove off, heading north.

Grober gave him a few seconds' head start, then followed. Hoping that Baylor kept the Porsche within the United States government's speed limit, which also happened to be the Pinto's.

Baylor did, and Grober followed him all the way into Santa Fe.

Baylor certainly wasn't acting like someone who had disappeared. First, he had a lavish dinner, alone, at the Sheraton on St. Francis Drive (Grober had salsa and chips and a couple of V.O. sodas at the bar). Then he drove to Victor's, on San Francisco, and savored one brandy, and then another (while Grober nursed two more V.O. sodas).

Grober was beginning to worry about the man's spotting him, so when Baylor drove to the Purple Hogan, Grober crept around to the empty alleyway in the back, and maintained surveillance through the small window that gave him a good view of the entire room. And it was here, at approximately one o'clock, that someone slammed him over the head with a locomotive.

"Well," said Danny, grudgingly, "your polygraph checks out." Because a police officer's brother was involved, the Department had used an outside polygraph expert, not their own, to verify Grober's story. "And Miss Gail should be here any minute."

"What about the Pinto and the gun?" Grober asked. "You lift any prints?" His head was pounding. He had just returned to Danny's office after spending two hours with Sergeant Munsen in the interrogation room.

Danny shook his head. "Both wiped clean."

"That makes sense, I shoot someone in my own car, with my own gun, and then wipe off the prints. The criminal mastermind at work."

Danny shook his head, sat back, stared up at the ceiling. "Jeez, Phil, how could you do this to me?"

"*You?*"

"Do you know how this is going to look on my record? My own brother, a suspect in a murder case. And not just any murder case. No. It turns out that we've been keeping an eye on this Baylor for the past two months. Hernandez, over in Narcotics, just spent ten minutes jumping on my tail."

"Yeah, my heart really bleeds for you and Hernandez. My troubles are zip compared to yours. I mean, hey, what's a little concussion, right? In another month or two I'll probably be able to eat solid food."

"The doctor that Munsen called in says you don't have a concussion."

"Yeah, well," said Grober, probing the lump on his skull with tentative fingers, "I'd like a second opinion."

"I've got a second opinion," Danny said. "You're a jerk."

Grober nodded. "For this, I used to stop the neighborhood bully from beating up on you when we were kids."

"Phil, when we were kids, you *were* the neighborhood bully."

Grober ignored that. "Narcotics, huh? What kind of drugs are we talking?"

"Coke."

"Yeah? So what was the deal?"

Danny made a sour face.

"Come on, Danny, I'm in this movie, too, remember."

Danny frowned. "The story was that Baylor had connections to some bigtime buyers down in Albuquerque. He was supposed to be there on a meet yesterday."

"If Narcotics was keeping an eye on him, then how come . . ." Grober paused, and then suddenly he laughed. "They lost him, didn't they? They tailed him to Albuquerque and then they lost him."

"He pulled a U-turn at an intersection downtown. He must've spotted them."

Grober laughed again. "That restaurant down in Coreyville. Did they know about that?"

Danny nodded. "They had a man there. The cook. But no one thought of getting in touch with him, and he was under orders not to break cover."

"That's really terrific teamwork there, Danny."

Danny grunted. "It was Hernandez, not me."

"What about Baylor's car? The Porsche? You found that yet?"

"It was still in the lot at the Purple Hogan. A forensics crew just finished tearing it apart. Clean, no coke. Hernandez thinks whoever killed Baylor ripped it off. If it ever existed."

"Some dealer killed him?" Grober shook his head. "No. It was that woman down in Coreyville. Bonnie Little."

Danny looked at him.

"First of all," said Grober, "how would a dealer know that I had any connection to Baylor? Why would he sap me in the alley?"

"Why would Little?"

"She knew I was hanging around, looking for him, and she wanted to get to him without me seeing her."

"How'd she know you were in the alley?"

"She recognized my car in the lot. She must've made me when I was in the Pinto watching her restaurant. She saw the car, and knew I had to be hanging around somewhere. Maybe she was coming into the alley to use that window, the way I did."

"Uh-huh. And how did she know that Baylor would be at the Purple Hogan?"

"Maybe they'd arranged to meet there, earlier. Besides, a guy like Baylor, rich, how many places would he go to in Santa Fe? Three, maybe? Four? All she had to do was drive around, check them out until she found the Porsche."

"Assuming she knew he was in Santa Fe at all."

"Obviously, she did."

"Oh yeah. Obviously. Tell me this, Phil. Why'd she steal the Pinto?"

"She went through my pockets, she found my gun. She decided to dust him. She drives a motorcycle, Danny. That's not the best thing to use if you want to blow someone away in private."

"Why'd she go through your pockets?"

"How do I know? You're the cop, you find out. Danny, she's the only person involved in this who could've known that the keys in my pocket fit the Pinto."

Danny shook his head in mock admiration. "Amazing, Phil. I really don't know how the Department gets along without your help. Have you worked out a motive yet? I'd be real honored if you'd share it with me."

"There's gotta be one."

Danny nodded. "Yeah, generally. So suppose you tell me why Bonnie Little shot Hubbard Baylor, when the two of them got married just a week ago."

"They got *what?*"

"Married."

As Grober was assimilating this, someone knocked at Danny's door.

"Come in," Danny called out.

A woman entered. She was somewhere between fifty and sixty years old, and somewhere between two hundred and three hundred pounds. She wore sandals, a lemon-yellow caftan, and a broad-brimmed flowered hat atop an explosion of bright red hair. She turned from Grober to Danny and said, "I'm supposed to see a Lieutenant Grober?"

Danny stood up. "Yes, ma'am?"

"I'm Winnifred Gail."

Danny looked at Grober. Grober closed his mouth, which had dropped open. He sighed and said, "It figures."

Winnifred Gail knocked back the shooter of fifteen-year-old bourbon in one gulp and then, sighing happily, plopped her heavy body back in her chair. "So you think it was Bonnie Little."

Sitting on the padded leather ottoman opposite her desk, a slab of three-inch glass maybe eight feet wide, Grober sipped at his shot glass. "The police think so, too. Sergeant Munsen asked the sheriff's department to bring her in for questioning."

Winnifred Gail refilled her glass from the bottle standing on a copy of *Art Space* magazine. "Well," she said, "it doesn't really surprise me. She's an artist. Painter. She may run a restaurant, but she thinks of herself as an artist. And artists are all nuts." She turned slightly in the chair, indicated with her shot glass the painting that hung on the wall behind her; it looked, to Grober, like two whoopee cushions mating. "That thing. Man who did it nearly killed his girlfriend last year. She started to hum while he was working, and he went bonkers. Tried to strangle her with his jump rope." She shook her head. "Lunatics, the whole bunch."

"Yeah, but why would Little kill Baylor?"

She shrugged. "Bonnie was the jealous type, I'd heard. Maybe *she* heard he was playing around."

"Was he?"

She shook her head. "Don't think so. He used to. Used to be famous for it. Different sweetie every month, and usually a little something on the side. But the way I hear it, he straightened up after he got involved with Bonnie. Went real domestic. They took turns staying at each other's place, and they were building a house down in Cerrillos, between here and Coreyville. Hubbard just put his own house up for sale last week."

"What did he do, Baylor?"

"Do? For a living? Nothing. He didn't have to. Wealthy family, trust fund. If you asked him, he'd tell you he was in investments. Which was true, in a way—but they were all his daddy's."

"The police think he was dealing coke."

"Nah. Oh, he sold some now and then, but he gave away most of what he had. He never did it for the money, that's for sure. Didn't have to. Born with a silver spoon in his nose." She laughed, a short quick bark.

"Sounds like you knew him pretty well."

She shrugged. "I sell Indian artifacts. We've done business together, Hubbard and I. He was a collector. So was Bonnie—sold her a few pieces when she first came to town, a year ago. Their collections, that's what first brought them together. That, and their money."

"Money?" said Grober, surprised. "You mean Little's got money, too?"

"Sure. Another trust fund baby."

"Then how come she runs a restaurant? How come she goes around dressed like Walter Brennan?"

"Some rich folks are just plain embarrassed by their cash. Bonnie paints, she runs the restaurant, she does charity work. The money's not supposed to matter." She grinned. "Course, when it came to marrying, you'll notice she didn't pick herself a busboy."

"And you say she was the jealous type?"

"Yep."

"Who'd know about that?"

"Here in Santa Fe? Anyone. Everyone. This is a small town. Greenwich Village in the desert. Santa Fe produces four things—good art, bad art, good Mexican food, and dandy gossip. Everybody knows who's sleeping with whom, and who isn't, and why. Don't get me wrong. I wouldn't have it any other way." She barked again. "A girl's got to have *some* fun."

"It'd be my guess," Grober grinned, "that you get more than some."

She grinned back. "Buttering me up, huh? Good. Good technique." She eyed him speculatively. "Shame you're not twenty years younger."

Grober shrugged. "I didn't look any better then."

She barked. "It's not the looks, honey, it's the stamina."

"I gave up stamina when I was twelve. It was wearing me out."

Another bark. "Here. Have some more of this good bourbon. Build up your strength."

"Is that a threat?" Grober asked her as she refilled his glass.

She barked again. "Take it any way you want."

Grober decided that the safest thing to do was to ignore it. He said, "This woman who came to my office and said she was you. She told me that Baylor had stolen some piece of Hopi art from her. A *talot*-something. Made out of cottonwood root."

"A *talaotsumsime?*" Still another bark. "Pulling your leg, honey. There are only four of them in the whole world, and they were all stolen last year from Shungopavi—that's the shrine on the Hopi second mesa, in Arizona. No dealer in his right mind—no reputable dealer, anyway—would touch one of those. The FBI's been tracking them since last December. And I know a Hopi or two, right here in town, who'd be happy to cut your throat if he thought you had one. Hopis are generally a real peaceful people, but those things were used in a couple of their most important rituals, and they're irreplaceable, the rituals can't be performed without them. The Hopis are pretty disturbed."

"Would she have to be an art dealer to know about them?"

"Not here in Santa Fe. We're all experts here."

"Why do you figure she used your name?"

She shrugged. "If she wanted to run this Hopi scam on you, I'm the only game in town. There are only two well-known dealers of ancient Indian artifacts in Santa Fe, and she would've had a real hard time impersonating Sam Taylor. He's five feet tall and bald as a honeydew melon. About as smart, too. What'd this bimbo look like, anyway?"

Grober described her.

"Skinny, huh," she said. "Well, some are built for speed." She leered over her shot glass. "And some are built for comfort."

Grober decided to ignore that, as well. "Do you know her?"

She shook her head. "Don't think so. No one around here dressed like that. Except at Halloween."

"She talked," Grober said, "like she went to one of those women's colleges back east. Vassar, Bryn Mawr. Like she had a mouth full of marbles."

"Nope . . . Oh. Of course. Of *course*. That *witch*. Wait, I think I've even got a picture."

She got up, walked to a file cabinet, pulled out a drawer. "Back issue of *Southwest Art*," she said. "I think, let me see, I think it was last December. Big opening over on Canyon Road. Here." She slipped out a magazine, opened it, riffled through the pages. "Hah. Score one for the large lady."

She came over to Grober and laid the opened magazine on his lap. "That her?"

Grober nodded. "That's her."

She was wearing black slacks and a gray silk blouse when she opened the heavy hardwood door. Her hair was shoulder length now, but Grober, having seen her photograph, was expecting that; she had worn a wig when she came to his office.

The moment she saw him, her face tightened and she reached out for the door again. Grober rammed his foot against its bottom.

"Hi," he said. "You come here often?"

Her upper lip curled back. "I could call the police."

Grober grinned. "That'll be swell."

She glared at him.

"It won't take long," he said. "I only want to fill in a few details."

Abruptly, wordlessly, she spun around and stalked down the hallway, her heels clicking on the red tiling. Grober followed her, pushing the door shut behind him.

She crossed the living room and stopped before the broad expanse of window, her back to Grober. She folded her arms beneath her breasts and looked down at the city of Santa Fe, the mountains far beyond turning pink now as the sun set.

It was an enormous room. A twelve foot high ceiling, supported by carefully oiled *vigas,* beams of straight pine log. Persian carpets, a long white sectional couch, leather chairs, a huge fieldstone fireplace.

"Verritt," Grober said. "Monica Verritt. That right?"

She said nothing.

"Did you hear the news?" Grober asked. "It was on the radio a while ago. Bonnie Little just confessed to shooting Hubbard Baylor."

She turned to face him. "What do you want?"

"Just a talk. Why don't you sit down."

Her eyes narrowed. "Blackmail. Is that it?" Suddenly her face relaxed; she laughed. "You sad, deluded little man. You haven't a prayer of getting a dime from me."

Grober shook his head. "No blackmail."

"I've done nothing wrong. I have absolutely no moral responsibility for what happened."

"Moral responsibility," Grober nodded. "Nice."

"And even if I had, whose word do you think the police will accept? *Mine,* or that of some fat, sleazy private detective?"

Grober sighed. "Sit down, lady, and shut up, so I can get this over and get out of here."

She sucked in a breath, let it out, then walked to the couch and sat down, her back rigid. "You have ten minutes."

"Terrific." He sat down opposite her in a leather chair. He said, "Six months ago, you and Hubbard Baylor were an item. Lot of people thought the two of you were going to make it permanent. So did you. But he dumped you, and after a while he took up with Bonnie Little. You didn't like that. You've got a pretty large idea of who you are—rich widow, patron of the arts, very hot stuff here in Santa Fe—and the idea of Baylor and Little didn't sit too good with you."

She leaned forward, opened a small mahogany box on the coffee table, removed from it a thin brown cigarette. "You appear," she said, "to have become a mine of information about me."

"I had a talk with Winnifred Gail. The real one."

She lit the cigarette, blew a cone of blue smoke toward the floor. "That absurd old hag. She's pathetic. She buys young boys, did you know that?"

Grober shrugged. "Not much point in buying old ones.

"Anyway, it didn't sit any better with you when Baylor and Little got married. You decided to do something about it."

With thumb and ring finger she plucked a tobacco flake from her lower lip. She smiled blandly. "Did I?"

"You came up with a plan. You couldn't use a local—everyone here in Santa Fe knows everyone else. And you needed an airhead, someone who didn't know what the deal was, someone who'd take in all the smoke you put out about Hopis and missing art. So you found me. You gave me that picture of you and Baylor, told me it was taken a week ago, told me I should use it to prove I was Baylor's friend. There was maybe a fifty-fifty chance I'd have to show it, but you figured that if I did, Little would go off the beam. You knew she was goofy with jealousy."

"There's virtually no way I could have anticipated what happened."

"Yeah. When you toss a spannner into a diesel engine, you never know what's gonna go first. And here's some other stuff you couldn't know. I talked to the cops before I came here. Little clubbed me over the head outside the Purple Hogan. When she was looking for the picture you gave me—she wanted to throw it in his face, she says—she found my gun. She took it along. To scare him into telling the truth. She also took my car—she didn't want to talk to him in the Porsche. That was his territory, she says. Sounds loopy to me, but I don't think she had all her oars in the water right then."

Grober crossed his legs. "Anyway, Little picked him up and drove him a few blocks away, showed him the photograph, pulled out the gun. Baylor denied having anything to do with you. But here's the cute part. It turns out that he *was* playing around, with some cutie down in Albuquerque. He went down there yesterday for a couple of hours of slap and tickle.

"The cops were following him at the time—they were looking for a cocaine bust. Baylor spotted the tail and lost it—he thought it was Little, or someone hired by Little, checking up on him. Pretty funny, huh? Everybody was running around in circles yesterday. Slapstick city."

Monica Verritt didn't smile. She said, "So you see he *was* unfaithful. He deserved to die."

"Maybe. He probably had a different opinion. But he didn't have all his oars in the water either, it looks like, because he told all this to Little while she was holding a gun on him. And she shot him."

Monica Verritt raised her cigarette, inhaled on it, and blew a languid plume of smoke toward Grober. "She's thoroughly insane. I warned Hubbard about her."

"Yeah," he said. "I bet you did."

She flicked the cigarette lightly against the ashtray. "Are you quite finished now?"

"Almost."

"Good. This has all been rather tedious."

"Nah," Grober said, shaking his head. "The tedious part doesn't start till we get to court."

She raised an eyebrow. "To court?"

"Sure. The cops got a confession from Little, so her lawyer, whoever he is, even if he's some total doofus hot out of law school, he's bound to shoot for temporary insanity. Since I'm the guy who set things in motion, I'll be subpoenaed to testify. And naturally, I'll have to tell them about you."

She smiled. "They'll never believe you, you know. I have a certain standing in this community."

"Not then you won't. Not after the lawsuits."

She laughed, lightly, musically. *"Lawsuits?"*

"Mine and Winnifred Gail's. She's suing you for punitive damages because you used her name. It's not illegal to impersonate an art dealer." As Winnifred Gail had said, and barked with laughter, a lot of people did that in Santa Fe. "But it is illegal to impersonate a *particular* art dealer, or any particular business owner, and sign his name to a contract. It also leaves you open to civil suit. Section 55 of the Criminal Code, Article 3, Paragraph 405. I looked it up."

"How enterprising of you." She smiled, clearly entertained. "And you're suing me as well, are you?"

"Right. It was me you signed the contract with. For one week, at a hundred and fifty per diem. You paid an advance of three hundred, but never paid the balance."

She sat back, her smile widening. "So it *is* blackmail. Or a pitiful attempt at it."

Grober shook his head. "No. I don't want your money. I'd rather sue. That way, I can collect punitive damages, just like Winnifred Gail."

"Ah, but you seem to be forgetting something. How are you going to prove that I did any of this?"

"You're the one forgetting things. Your handwriting is on the contract. Your prints are all over my office. And remember that picture you gave me, of you and Hubbard Baylor? The cops have it now. Your prints are on that, too, and so are mine. All of it will come out at your trial."

"My trial?" Surprised, and no longer smiling.

"Right. The one for fraud and forgery. Winnifred Gail and I already went to the cops with all this. They're drawing up a warrant right now."

Once again she laughed, but now the music had drained away, leaving the laughter hollow and brittle. "You can't be serious."

Grober nodded. "Sure I can."

She leaned forward, carefully put out her cigarette. She looked up at him. "It'll never get to court."

Grober shrugged. "Maybe not. But maybe it will. And it'll definitely get to the newspapers. With that, and with the civil suits, mine and Winnifred Gail's, by the time Bonnie Little comes to trial, your swell standing in the community will be lying down, flat on its back. You know, I wouldn't really be surprised if she got an acquittal. Young artist, just married, jerked around by a nasty older woman. That's the way I'd go, if I were her lawyer."

Monica Verritt sat back, crossed her arms beneath her breasts "Why?" she said. "Why are you doing this?"

Grober said, "Winnifred Gail's doing it because she doesn't like you. Come right down to it, I don't think very many people do. I know I don't. You used me. *I* was the spanner." He shrugged. "Like you said in my office. It's a matter of pride."

Her lip curled. *"Pride."*

"Yeah," he said. "There's a lot of it going around." He stood up, turned, and walked away, across the Persian carpet.

He had almost reached the front door when, behind him, at the end of the hallway, she shouted, calling him a particularly unpleasant name. He wheeled around in time to see the cigarette box come spinning toward his head. He ducked; it shattered against the door, thin brown cigarettes flying everywhere. He looked back at her.

She stood there, breathing heavily, arms limp at her sides. Then her face screwed up and she spat the name again. But more softly now, and with spite rather than fury, and the spite hopeless and empty, like a wounded child's.

"Right," Grober said. "See you in court." He opened the door and stepped into the night.

Bibliography

Cocaine Blues (Dell, 1980)

The Aegean Affair (Dell, 1982)

The Short Stories, *Alfred Hitchcock's Mystery Magazine*
"A Conflict of Interest," November 1982
"To Catch a Wizard," March 1983
"A Matter of Pride," April 1984
"A Greek Game," May 1985
"The Motor Coach of Allah," December 1985
"Make No Mistake," June 1989
"The Gold of Miyani," Winter 1989
"The Smoke People"

Wall of Glass (St. Martin's, 1987), 2,500 copies

Miss Lizzie (St. Martin's, 1989), 5,000 copies

At Ease with the Dead (St. Martin's, 1990), 5,000 copies

Wilde West (St. Martin's, 1991), 6,000 copies

Flower in the Desert (St. Martin's, 1992), 6,000 copies

The Hanged Man (St. Martin's, 1993), in press